MW01030162

CO-PARENTING
FROM THE
INSIDE OUT

Karen Kristjanson

KAREN L. KRISTJANSON

CO-PARENTING FROM THE INSIDE OUT

Voices of Moms and Dads

DUNDURN
TORONTO

Cover image: istock.com/Nastco
Printer: Webcom

Library and Archives Canada Cataloguing in Publication

Kristjanson, Karen L., author
    Co-parenting from the inside out : voices of moms and
dads / Karen L. Kristjanson.

Includes bibliographical references.
Issued in print and electronic formats.
ISBN 978-1-4597-4057-0 (softcover).--ISBN 978-1-4597-4058-7 (PDF).--
ISBN 978-1-4597-4059-4 (EPUB)

    1. Parenting, Part-time. 2. Single parents. 3. Mothers--Interviews.
4. Fathers--Interviews. I. Title.

HQ759.915.K75 2017   649'.1   C2017-905863-0
                                                    C2017-905864-9

1 2 3 4 5   21 20 19 18 17

Conseil des Arts du Canada   Canada Council for the Arts   Canadä

ONTARIO ARTS COUNCIL
CONSEIL DES ARTS DE L'ONTARIO
an Ontario government agency
un organisme du gouvernement de l'Ontario

We acknowledge the support of the Canada Council for the Arts, which last year invested $153 million to bring the arts to Canadians throughout the country, and the **Ontario Arts Council** for our publishing program. We also acknowledge the financial support of the **Government of Ontario**, through the **Ontario Book Publishing Tax Credit** and the **Ontario Media Development Corporation**, and the **Government of Canada**.

Nous remercions le **Conseil des arts du Canada** de son soutien. L'an dernier, le Conseil a investi 153 millions de dollars pour mettre de l'art dans la vie des Canadiennes et des Canadiens de tout le pays.

Care has been taken to trace the ownership of copyright material used in this book. The author and the publisher welcome any information enabling them to rectify any references or credits in subsequent editions.
                                    — *J. Kirk Howard, President*

The publisher is not responsible for websites or their content unless they are owned by the publisher.

Printed and bound in Canada.

VISIT US AT

 dundurn.com | @dundurnpress | dundurnpress | dundurnpress

Dundurn
3 Church Street, Suite 500
Toronto, Ontario, Canada
M5E 1M2

For my sons,
David and Steven,
who always give me hope

CONTENTS

FOREWORD

I am honoured to write this foreword. Practical books of this calibre on the topic of shared parenting are scarce; the author's immersion into the now-vast literature on co-parenting and engagement with the material in a co-operative and collaborative manner has given birth to an extremely useful guide to addressing the challenges of parenting after divorce.

Children need both parents. Little else needs to be said. They also need responsible and responsive parenting, and parents who have good mental health and who remain child-focused. They need co-operative co-parenting, and to be shielded from parental conflict, which is tantamount to child abuse when children are exposed to it over a prolonged period.

This book will be invaluable when shared parenting becomes established as the norm in family laws internationally. A legal presumption of shared parenting, rebuttable in cases of family violence, is a corollary of the National Association of Women and the Law's recommendation of a legal presumption against shared parenting in situations of family violence. We now know from the research that shared parenting, absent family violence, is not only in the best interests of children, but is associated with significantly better physical and mental health outcomes for both mothers and fathers.

In the realm of parenting after divorce, each situation is unique. Yet the law is a blunt instrument when it comes to post-divorce living arrangements, and is dependent on idiosyncratic and biased judgments in an area in which judges have little or no expertise. Shared parenting provides an opportunity for parents to tailor living arrangements to the unique needs of their children. This book provides a solid foundation for co-parents from the beginning.

As with so many arenas of child and family policy and practice, there is no shortage of controversy in regard to post-divorce parenting. Ideas such as shared parenting are considered radical and marginalized by an establishment that gains from preserving the status quo.

The current norm, which involves the forced disengagement of divorced parents from children's lives via primary residence court orders, has resulted in a precipitous decline in the amount of time parents are able to spend with their children in two-parent families. Yet we encourage and expect shared parenting in most two-parent families today, and this is the choice of more parents, as mothers are working outside the home to the same degree as fathers. Shared parenting in two-parent families is alive and well, as fathers and mothers share both the joys and burdens of parenthood, and the rewards and challenges of an outside work environment.

As stated above, children need their parents, and they need both of their parents. Every situation is unique, but whatever the circumstance, children have similar needs, according to their age and stage of development. When parents are sensitive, attuned, and responsive to their children's needs, children feel secure and will adapt more easily to change.

As they are primarily responsible for their children's needs, parents also need the support of community and social systems. It is the responsibility of social institutions to support parents in the fulfillment of their parental responsibilities, including co-parental responsibilities. It is unacceptable that for many families, representatives of social institutions, such as the legal, child welfare, and educational systems, undermine rather than support parents in the fulfillment of their parental responsibilities. (Nowhere is this more evident than in the realm of adversarial family law.)

Therapeutic family mediation focused on children's needs in the development of a co-operative co-parenting plan, set in the context of a legal presumption that children need both parents in their lives for their optimal well-being, offers a viable alternative to the current adversarial system.

Child focus should be the key element and primary consideration in family mediation and negotiation focused on the development of a co-parenting plan. Looking at divorce through the eyes of one's children is a *sine qua non* in effective parental communication and connection with children during and after the divorce transition. Children of different ages and stages of development will have different needs and capacities that can be drawn upon to build resilience. Giving children a voice requires openness and sensitivity. Active listening reassures children that they are being heard and understood; it can also help children to name their feelings. Building their understanding of the divorce over time gives children a way to grasp the situation, and opens the door to giving children and adolescents a say in their lives.

Despite the lip service being paid to the critical importance of the "best interests of the child" principle in divorce proceedings, rarely (if ever) are children themselves allowed the opportunity to voice their views on the matter of their best interests. Many experts claim to know what children want and desire, but this knowledge is based more on speculation and interpretation and less on the recognition that children themselves are, in a very real sense, the true experts on their own best interests, as they are the most affected by their parents' divorce. These "expert" pronouncements effectively silence children and render them mute in divorce proceedings.

My simple but constant plea, a mantra, to divorce practitioners and policymakers is that we adopt a new standard in the legal determination of parenting after divorce: the "best interests of the child from the perspective of the child," to replace the current discretionary approach based on speculation and interpretation; and a "responsibility to needs-based" orientation, to replace the dominant "rights-based" approach.

Two key factors stand out in regard to children's adjustment to the consequences of divorce: protecting children from conflict and preserving their relationships with both parents.

One of the best things parents can do to protect their children from the negative consequences of parental separation and to help them thrive is one of the most difficult — reducing conflict between parents. A high degree of inter-parental conflict nearly always results in difficulties for children, as children are profoundly affected by how their parents handle conflict.

One of the most damaging forms of child abuse is parental aliena-tion. Parental alienation involves the "programming" of a child by one parent to denigrate the other parent, in an effort to undermine and inter-fere with the child's relationship with that parent, and is often a sign of a parent's inability to separate from the couple conflict and focus on the needs of the child. Parental alienation produces a mental condition in which a child allies him- or herself with an alienating parent and rejects a relationship with the other parent without legitimate justification. The severe effects of parental alienation on children are well-documented: low self-esteem and self-hatred, lack of trust, depression, and substance abuse and other forms of addiction are widespread, as children lose the capacity to give and accept love from a parent.

Maintaining relationships between children and both parents and good co-parenting protects children from risk, and is the key element in building resilient children who have experienced their parents' divorce. The vast majority of children do better when they have a meaningful relationship with both parents. Children in shared parenting arrange-ments have fewer conduct and emotional problems, higher self-esteem, and better family relations and school performance than children who live in sole custody arrangements. The capacity of parents to co-operate increases in shared parenting arrangements, and decreases in sole-custody arrangements.

A co-parenting plan provides parents with a management tool to enable successful shared parenting. A co-parenting plan, developed with the best interests of the children in mind, lays out how children will spend time with each parent; how parents will make decisions about their chil-dren; how parents will exchange information and communicate about their children; how parents will handle appointments and extracurricu-lar arrangements for their children; and how parents will resolve dis-putes. Parents communicate in a businesslike fashion only about issues directly related to the children. Research tells us that over time and as the dust settles, parallel parenting sets the stage for co-operative parenting.

This book does not supply all the answers in regard to the challenges of co-parenting. More importantly, however, it asks the right questions, such as those related to co-parenting in the context of addiction and mental health challenges. It focuses on strategies designed to maximize the routine involvement of both parents for children at different ages and stages of development, while at the same time protecting children from the ravages of parental conflict and the threat of family violence.

In addition, the voices of parents themselves are interwoven throughout the text and provide real-life examples of effective problem-solving that will provide inspiration to parents who are struggling with how to maintain their own well-being while keeping a primary focus on the needs of their children. These parents are the pioneers in what is now an international social movement, the shared parenting approach to meeting the needs and best interests of children in the divorce transition. Their wisdom and insights provide a critical aspect of this book, which represents an important contribution to our collective understanding of how best to address children's core needs, as well as enhancing their parents' well-being during what is the most stressful period in the lives of many families.

Edward Kruk, author of *Divorce and Disengagement, Mediation and Conflict Resolution in Social Work and the Human Services, Divorced Fathers*, and *The Equal Parent Presumption*, is a specialist in child and family policy. He teaches at the University of British Columbia, where he is an associate professor of social work.

INTRODUCTION

Welcome to co-parenting after divorce. This isn't a world we dreamed about when we were young. Our world has not unfolded as we wished. But it's real. Once we arrive, willingly or not, we must reshape our former patterns of living and parenting. Even more than before, we know our actions will create our children's future.

Co-parenting my sons, David and Steven, I often felt anxious and alone. I had no mentors or maps to show me how to raise the boys so they could have a deep relationship with both me and their dad, in our separate homes. Like many other parents, I didn't want my children to be hurt by their parents' choices.

Sharing parenting in those early days was exhausting; it was hard to know if I was doing the right things. My familiar ways of functioning weren't relevant now. I often turned to books to sustain me and remind me that I wasn't the only person struggling, even when my colleagues and neighbours looked like they had it all together. Books gave me new ways to think about things when my mind spun anxiously, *I have to make this work! Now!* They refreshed my spirit and fortified me with new energy.

One evening I was reading Oriah Mountain Dreamer's book *The Dance: Moving to the Rhythms of Your True Self*. I was drinking in her open, loving style, not expecting any lightning bolts of insight. She wrote how she felt helping her grown sons prepare to take part in their dad's remarriage ceremony. The day of the wedding, her son asks for her help in choosing a poem to recite.

"I do not point out that he has had days, if not weeks, to prepare for this, that this is supposed to be my Saturday alone, that I have work if not a life to attend to, and that it is at least a little weird for me to be finding a poem for a toast at my ex-husband's wedding. I don't really want to have anything to do with this. It has nothing to do with me. But it is happening in their lives, and so it is happening in mine."*

The power of her words amazed me. I was not alone! Others had experienced these messy, bittersweet feelings and grappled with how to support their children with grace through awkward events. Something deep in me relaxed.

I had never seen this kind of story written down. I wanted more. I thought, *There should be a book of these stories, where co-parents can learn how others feel and think as they go through all this. Well, I have lived this journey myself. As a life coach with two master's degrees and decades of experience in human relations work, I will write it.*

That was more than a decade ago. I was working and sharing parenting with no room in my life for writing. My sons are now grown; at twenty-eight and thirty-one, they are good men. My conviction that co-parenting can be a sound choice continues to grow.

What Is Co-Parenting?

Here is my definition.

The heart of co-parenting or shared parenting is the relationship between separated/divorced parents and their children. It is sharing everyday routines as well as holidays so that both parents are meaningfully involved in their children's lives. It lets parents stay in tune with their children's growth, needs, and potential; children experience their parents in a range of times and settings. It isn't important that time be divided equally — 30 percent can be enough — but that the children take part in the regular rhythms of life with both parents.

There are many options for co-parenting. Here are examples:

- Monday/Wednesday/Friday with one parent, the remaining days with the other

---

*Oriah Mountain Dreamer, *The Dance: Moving to the Rhythms of Your True Self* (New York: HarperCollins, 2001), 98.

- three weekends per month plus one weekday evening each week with one parent, the rest with the other parent
- Tuesday to Saturday morning with one parent, Saturday afternoon to Monday night with the other

A co-parent is *not*, for instance, a parent who sees the children one or two weekends each month. That won't give the mom or dad much sense of their children's weekly routines and how they respond to daily demands and rewards. Nor will the children get a rounded sense of who that parent is. A relationship consisting of weekly Skype calls isn't co-parenting, either. While wonderful connections can be made, it's not the whole tamale of parenting: helping, setting expectations, hugging, eating together, and random acts of togetherness.

The stories that follow feature parents who had care of their children between 30 and 70 percent of the time for at least a few years.

Is This Book for You?

This book is called *Co-Parenting from the Inside Out* because it contains kernels of insight and encouragement gleaned from co-parents' experiences. It is written for mothers and fathers who are sharing parenting, or considering it. Because parents need help from family, lawyers, mediators, teachers, therapists, and coaches, this book will also help people in supporting roles. Children who have been co-parented may understand their parents' world and decisions more fully.

If you are co-parenting

- you will find here some of your own thoughts, feelings, and experiences, and hearing others' journeys will reassure you that you are not alone;
- you will gain a broader perspective on your situation by seeing the inside view of others' experiences;
- you will see new possibilities for action, and things to avoid; and
- you'll feel like you have sat down with a support group of parents who are open about saying, "This is what co-parenting was for me."

Because many stories include how the children fared as they grew, you will gain hope that what you are doing can move you and your children forward in a good direction; that co-parenting, while often hard, is important and worthwhile.

If you are separating, divorcing, or considering co-parenting

- you will understand how others have made choices in situations like yours, what they did, and what happened next;
- you will learn helpful strategies;
- you will make more thoughtful decisions because your perspective has broadened; and
- you will develop more confidence in your future and your children's futures.

If you are supporting someone who is co-parenting

- you will gain insight into their world;
- you'll have a deeper understanding of their feelings and thoughts;
- you will see opportunities to assist parents in unforeseen ways; and
- you will feel more confident in discerning what actions may be helpful, or not.

Co-Parenting from the Inside Out is not full of quick answers. Stories offer a richness more textured and individual than crisp advice on how to do things. They open up the inner worlds of mothers and fathers living the messy complexities of co-parenting after divorce. They give perspectives about what's important and ideas of what's possible. Many stories reveal courage, love, and growth.

With time and parents' determination, many good things happened in these families. There is a lot of pain here, too; splitting up a family is not a happy event. Yet many mothers and fathers found ways not only to survive but also to persevere and find new possibilities for themselves and their children. You may, as I did, find them inspiring.

Whose Stories Are These?

The mothers and fathers interviewed were living across the United States and Western Canada. I sought parents in widely diverse circumstances, finding them by word of mouth and through the internet. Facebook and Twitter contacts, friends, coaching colleagues, and family members provided names of possible interviewees. A local paper published an article about the project, and readers emailed me to volunteer their stories.

I developed a template of questions to use, and refined it with help from psychologist Dr. Leigh Bowie. You will find the full set of questions in Appendix 1.

The forty-two parents who told their stories ranged in age from twenty-seven to sixty-five. Some were straight, some gay. Some struggled financially, some were well off. Some endured high-conflict situations, while others had minimal strife in their separation and divorce. Some parents had children with special needs, and some parents themselves had mental health problems. Fourteen were fathers and twenty-eight, mothers.

Some parents were in their first year of separation, still in the throes of surging feelings. Many were in the first ten years past divorce. Others had children grown and independent; they looked years back for their memories. Each story gave a snapshot of that parent's view at the time we spoke. Those perspectives, too, will have evolved since then. People's perceptions of their experiences shift and often become broader with the passage of time.

Moms and dads make hundreds of decisions each day: Do I have time to listen more here? Do I need to take a firm line? What does my child need right now? It is so hard to tell whether any decision is a good one. As Brené Brown says, "Parenting is our wildest adventure in vulnerability."* I deeply appreciated the openness of those interviewed. They revealed their struggles and uncertainties as they made daily choices. I have changed names and details in the stories to preserve anonymity except in the next chapter, which contains my own experience.

---

*Brené Brown, *The Gifts of Imperfect Parenting: Raising Children with Courage, Compassion, and Connection* (Louisville, CO: Sounds True, 2013), Audiobook, 2 compact discs.

Co-Parenting Isn't for Everyone

Co-Parenting from the Inside Out is written for those doing or considering co-parenting, but that does not mean co-parenting is always best. Parents need to assess their individual situation. In cases of physical or sexual abuse of a parent or child, co-parenting will be a bad choice. If you have concerns about your children's safety, find a therapist or other specialist in family issues and have a frank discussion about your options.

The Link Between Co-Parenting and Growth

As I immersed myself in others' experiences, growth kept showing up. It helped both parents and children. Parents grew, partly just through living each day. Most found sources of support: journal writing, books, friends and family, therapists, counsellors, or coaches. Almost all the parents interviewed developed new strengths, insights, and confidence. As they expanded their skills and perspectives, they were better able to nurture their children.

Another appealing feature of growth emerged: you have some say in it. By the time you're facing the need to share parenting, you may have little control over many aspects of your life. What your former partner wants and does, your own and your children's health, your financial situation … it's a long list. One area where you *do* have some control is how you support your own growth. You have many options.

Growth means a lot to me because my life's work has been helping people develop and change. As a school psychologist, leadership trainer, change consultant, and life/leadership coach, I have supported people for thirty years in finding ways to grow and reach their goals. My journey from being a mother in a two-parent family to co-parenting my sons after divorce stretched me in countless ways. I gradually developed new depths of compassion, resilience, and confidence.

How to Get the Most from This Book

You have choices in where to go from here; you can read straight through or jump to where your curiosity leads you. The next chapter tells my story and reflects my individual perspective on events. Ten chapters of shorter stories follow. Chapter 2 shows the wide range of co-parenting arrangements that people have lived. It includes suggestions on how to step back from your family situation and gain a broader perspective. Give the ideas a try; even the smallest shift in your perceptions can make a difference.

Chapter 3 offers tips on the critical skill of making good decisions during emotionally charged times. Its stories illustrate how decisions, wise or unwise, weave through co-parenting.

Most chapters focus on one kind of experience, such as addictions or high conflict or growth or lesbian couples, though all stories contain a variety of elements. Keywords at the beginning story give extra clues about its unique factors. You can go right to the chapters or stories that interest you most.

Every story here gives a partial view of reality, and as you read you will have reactions. You may think, "Wow, what a brave choice!" or "I would *never* do that!" Parents in circumstances most similar to yours may evoke the strongest feelings. Try to notice your reactions. They will help you understand your own values and choices more clearly. Look for what helped these parents make wise decisions and grow.

Those who want the big picture first can start with the last two chapters. Chapter 12 lists specific positive actions that parents, institutions, and families can take. Chapter 13 reveals the overall lessons I drew from the interviews.

The appendices give more information about the interviews and offer other co-parenting resources.

I wish you every good fortune.

My Story:
One Foot in Front
of the Other

The crack in your heart allows light in.
— LESLIE BRATSPIS

I heaved my suitcase into the back of my rusted Corolla and sank into the driver's seat. I was parked in the driveway of the suburban Winnipeg house where I had become the mother of two sons, then aged five and eight. On that November night the curbs were edged with dusty snow, the brown lawns sullen and hard. On that night I was leaving my home and my marriage of fifteen years.

I backed onto the street and drove around the curve, crying so hard I couldn't see. As soon as I was out of sight of the house, I pulled over, sobbing, my head in my arms on the cold steering wheel. My sons, David and Steven, had known for a week that my husband, John, and I were separating, but this was the first tangible step to reshaping our family. I knew their dad would care well for them that night. Still, it had taken every ounce of my resolve to kneel, look into their sad, bewildered faces, and hug them goodbye, saying, "I will see you tomorrow." Leaving the house was such a significant step, it felt unreal and desperate. After a few bleak minutes, I took a shaky breath, restarted the car, and drove slowly out of the neighbourhood toward my temporary refuge.

The ship that had been my married life had foundered and I was throwing myself into black, cold water. I didn't know how this next phase would work, just that our family life as it was couldn't continue.

In the previous year, I had realized that our marriage was frayed to the breaking point. Years of escalating arguments had led John and me to try counselling, but after three months, John stopped going. When I asked, "What is it that's not working for you?" he answered, "I just don't think it's going anywhere." It felt like I was standing on one side of a two-way mirror with John on the other side. He could see what I was experiencing, but my view of him was opaque, shielded. I felt more and more helpless, trying to peer through the glass. Very lonely.

Finally, one sunny Saturday morning, sitting across from each other in our matching blue wing chairs, we had our first honest talk in years. I comprehended what I hadn't wanted to see: John's commitment to our marriage was gone.

As this horrifying realization sank in, I felt like I had been punched in the belly. I spent that day sitting, walking, staring into space, trying to rearrange my world. We carried on for the next few weeks in an atmosphere charged with things unsaid as I gathered my nerve and looked at options. One thing was clear to me: while John would be content to carry on as before, as if nothing had changed, I could not. I peered briefly down that future path and saw myself there — a bitter, weary woman with no joy in living.

I started examining other choices. I knew the boys loved us both and would need time with each of us. For them to be brought up well, they would need parents who were healthy human beings. For me, in addition to lots of time with David and Steven, I would need time to myself each week, real downtime, or I would be a terrible mother — constantly shrewish and irritable. So, co-parenting seemed the least disastrous option. I confess I wasn't all that concerned about John's needs, but a part of me registered faintly that it would be good for him to keep connected with the boys.

I knew that John was good with David and Steven, that he loved them. Even through my haze of hurt and anger, I could see he had gifts to offer them, different than mine. I drove them to music lessons, curled up with them nightly to sing lullabies, and made sure they ate vegetables. He took them to his family farm and expected them to do physical labour, carried them on his shoulders, and got them giggling as he wrestled with them. Whatever else happened, John was the boys' father, and they needed to grow up knowing and taking pride in both of their parents. I never doubted the importance of this in the long term.

Once I actively began to consider leaving, I carried tension throughout my body, wondering if I could make good choices. My throat felt tight, my breathing shallow. I kept rolling my shoulders to try and loosen them. My work colleagues never gave advice, which I appreciated, but they saw me each morning haggard from lousy sleep. Puffy bags under my eyes made me look closer to sixty than forty. In our small office, sympathetic looks told me people knew I was grappling with whether to leave my marriage. For my fortieth birthday, co-workers threw a coffee party, covering my office ceiling with exuberant red and white helium balloons trailing ribbons. I almost cried at the absurdly cheerful sight. A colleague said, "You'll know what to do when the time comes." Her confidence helped me keep listening to myself to find my next steps. I needed every ounce of confidence-building that came my way.

John and I tiptoed around each other for weeks, keeping a buffer of politeness between us.

"Will you be able to take Steven to his practice tomorrow night?"

"Sure."

We seemed stuck, unable to go back or forward. I felt increasingly fragile, as if my inner core was dissolving in the endless effort to keep a normal facade.

Finally, one evening, as I was folding laundry in our bedroom, John came in. I suddenly couldn't do this any longer. I blurted, "If we separated, would you consider co-parenting?" I was scared to ask the question, as if naming the possibility of separating might make it more real. John didn't look at me.

After a few long seconds, his answer came: "Okay."

It was a huge relief to me. There was a viable, if terrifying, way forward.

No one I knew was co-parenting. Considering it felt odd, as if I were peering into strange new territory. I talked over the possibility with friends, but no one had done anything like it. I looked in bookstores, but at that time there was little on the shelves.

Co-parenting never felt like a good choice. I had wanted so much to keep the family together that anything else was a sad and scary unknown, something that didn't fit the dream of family. However, the dream was gone. Shared parenting offered the fewest bad outcomes.

When I asked myself if co-parenting would work, I started by assessing our resources. First, I felt fairly confident that I could earn a living if we split. It wouldn't be fancy, but we could survive. I also believed that John could stay solvent, so we each could provide some financial base. This was critical. Another factor was family support. My parents and siblings lived three thousand kilometres away in British Columbia. I wasn't willing to uproot myself and the boys, or ask them to choose between their dad and me, in order to move closer to my family. Therefore, their dad's relatives, right in Winnipeg, were an important resource. I felt genuine affection for his family and believed they would provide social support for both the boys and their dad.

Next, I needed to look at where I would live with the boys, and where their dad might live with them. I couldn't imagine staying in our house, with its echoes of heartache. I thought we should sell the house we jointly owned, both move to a nearby, less expensive neighbourhood, and find homes within walking distance of each other. John, on the other hand, first expected that I would stay in our house. When I said absolutely not, John announced he would stay there. He didn't want to introduce any more change into the boys' lives than they were already facing.

This turned out to be an excellent decision because it gave the boys social stability. I am grateful now that John insisted on staying in the house and that I didn't oppose him further. I can see how pain dominated my thinking, limiting my readiness to consider all options carefully.

What would it be like to see the boys only part of the week and have them move back and forth? I couldn't imagine what it would feel like for any of us. I supposed we would all survive, but beyond that it was uncharted territory.

First Steps

The very first step — telling the boys that we couldn't stay together — was horribly hard. John and I agreed we should talk to them together, so we called them into the kitchen. John and I looked at each other. This was the crunch point, and neither of us knew what to say. Finally, I forced the words out of my mouth: "Your dad and I have realized we can't live together anymore."

Steven, at age five, didn't understand what we meant, but eight-year-old David started to cry. Of course he was crying, we were ripping his world apart! We both kept saying that we still loved them and that they would still have both of us, but it felt like meaningless words drifting in the air. Things eased a bit when David started to ask specific questions, like what would happen next. But nothing could really soften the blow. We were destroying their world. It was the hardest thing I have ever done.

John and I agreed to keep changes to a minimum for six months and reconsider from there. We decided to keep the boys in the house for that time, and each take a turn moving out for three months. I left the house first because I was desperate to get things moving.

Through friends I found a basement apartment a fifteen-minute drive away. It was tiny, all I could afford, with a dingy loveseat and threadbare easy chair in the brown-painted living room. The windows were small, high, and dusty, opening at sidewalk level so even the mid-afternoon light struggled to filter through. I unpacked my suit-case, guitar, and some books, and looked around. I might as well have been on the moon. I took each of the first two nights one hour at a time, reading, crying, dozing, and bawling the Gordon Lightfoot song "For Lovin' Me," pounding on my guitar strings. When the phone was hooked up after three days, I felt calmer, linked to the boys and the outside world.

The apartment didn't inspire affection in me, but it was my refuge. The surrounding streets lined with quiet elms quickly drew me. I walked and cried and walked and cried. I tried to sort out this new reality, letting myself weep and rage as random memories triggered waves of feelings. I had loved John for many years and couldn't just turn that love off. It hurt over and over to try. My relieved-and-released self was only slightly bigger than my wailing-and-grieving self. I tried to let go of my dream of family. I pictured it starting out a glorious banner gleaming red and gold and green, diminishing with time, now lying stained and tattered on the ground.

Every day or two, I would drive over and get the boys, and take them either for an outing, to a hockey practice, or to my apartment for a visit. I spent time with them, fed them, and asked about school. I wanted to give them a sense of love and continuity, but I was so fragile myself that I didn't have much to offer beyond the basics.

I felt sweet relief to be free of the endless tension between John and me. My anger, though, came with me. I comforted myself at first with a fantasy of parading in front of John's office building with a condemnatory placard. How satisfying it would feel to embarrass him. My counsellor firmly discouraged that idea. Then I simply wished that he could disappear from the world. I didn't want to kill him (okay, there were a few flashes at first). I felt that if he were magically not there, the slag heap of anger inside me would disappear. But then I would remember how important he was to the boys and feel guilty. It was hard to talk with him face-to-face, because familiar tension would clamp down in my stomach, my shoulders, my jaw, and I would contract into a hard shell.

John and I said little to each other when meeting to transfer the boys. One of us might offer a few stilted sentences about a school event or homework. When standing inside the door of the house that had been ours, I felt raw and confused. Part of me felt right at home and ready to resume my old life, striding into the kitchen for a glass of water. The rest of me felt like an alien visitor, banished from my home. It was always a relief to me, and probably to John as well, when we finished an encounter.

In the first years we needed to sort out many details. I needed to distance myself emotionally from John in order to discuss how things would work. When tempers flared, we withdrew to avoid inflicting the anger on the boys. After a few days we could usually resume a discussion. It felt schizophrenic to be in such an interdependent relationship with someone in whom I had so little trust, on one level. Yet I believed he was sincerely committed to the boys' welfare, so I could and needed to trust him as their father.

After two months, a thought popped up and wouldn't leave me: *I am on fast-forward. I am on fast-forward.* My inner self couldn't keep pace with the massive outward shifts. I needed time to slow down and let everything sink in. I heard this message for a few days. Suddenly I realized that I was the only one who could give me what I needed. Standing firm against the raised eyebrows and dubious looks of friends and family, I quit my job.

This was a bold step. My savings were modest, and I knew I would need to support myself full-time and the boys half-time. I hadn't considered myself a risk-taker, but my deep longing to slow down fuelled my courage.

Once I had left my job, I felt lighter. With whole days to myself, I walked even more, read and reread my favourite self-help authors like Melody Beattie, wrote in my journal, and played my guitar. No longer did I have to act normal and professional every day. I treated myself to a train trip to Toronto for four days, where old friends welcomed me, pampered me, and reminded me of times in my life when I was whole. I let myself grieve for what John and I had shared. When I returned to Winnipeg, I started my turn as the live-in parent in the family home for three months. I wasn't recovered from the cataclysm, but the first overwhelming crash of feelings had passed.

Settling In to Co-Parenting

After six months it was clear our separation would continue. I felt shaky and stressed, yet the freedom from living in a stuck marriage felt like I had put down a boulder. John and I agreed that the boys were doing as well as they could and that co-parenting was the way to go, long-term.

We discussed week-on/week-off as a possible schedule, but that seemed too long to be separated from the boys. To keep it simple, splitting a week seemed best. I drafted up a weekly schedule, taking into account what I knew of all of our preferences and activities. Then John and I fine-tuned the draft. In it the boys spent about four days of the week with me and three days with him. Our similar expectations of splitting the time fairly equally helped so much; I think we were both relieved at how easily that part went. Then we had to prepare a separation agreement, including finances.

Talking money was the hardest. We could be civil on most topics, but when deciding who should pay for what, tempers flashed without warning. I would shove a bunch of feelings to one side and refuse to let them creep into the discussion, but it was a struggle. Several times one of us stomped out midway through a conversation. We knew there was no alternative, so we kept coming back until it was done.

I don't recall asking the boys what their opinions were in planning the separation. I didn't want them to have to express any preferences that might feel like they had to choose between Mom and Dad.

The legal system and lawyers loomed vaguely in the background. When we first split, my friends made dire references to the possible legal consequences of my leaving the family home. That scared me enough that I consulted a lawyer a few times. John had had an unsatisfying experience suing an employer and said he wouldn't involve lawyers here. This freed me from fear that he might do so. We muddled through mostly on our own.

Although our counselling sessions hadn't mended our marriage, they probably made us more able to listen to each other and resist taking cheap shots in discussions. These skills helped us make a more civil separation and avoid big legal bills.

After six months, I moved into a two-bedroom apartment in our neighbourhood. Given John's determination to stay in the house, this was the only option. It was hard for him financially to cover the whole house mortgage, and I wasn't wild about the apartment, but it was a start. We began long-term co-parenting.

The first months in the new apartment passed in a blur of sorting through clothes and school things to ensure the boys would have what they needed at both places, finalizing the division of our furniture and pictures, and reminding the boys often to take things to and from their dad's place.

I began seeing a woman at John's house when picking up or dropping off the boys. I felt acidic jealousy. Knowing someone else would act as hostess at John's annual New Year's party had me ranting on the phone to my brother.

He listened and said matter-of-factly, "You're separated now. It's his house and his right."

"I know," I admitted. It was irrational, but that burning stayed in my gut for some time.

I felt sad, guilty, angry at John, and angry at myself, all rolled up together. And tired! I kept journaling, calling friends to vent or cry, and telling myself it would get easier. Once or twice it felt so tough that I wondered, *had I known how hard this would be, would I still have done it?* I saw a counsellor every other week. She helped me pull out some of my squashed-down feelings of grief, shame, and anger and look at them in daylight. They didn't disappear, but gentled. Accepting that I was simply human and shared weaknesses with the rest of the world lightened my step.

Signs of Progress

Gradually, I began to glimpse clear sky through the storm. Steven started to lose his pinched look and laugh more often. The three of us started to have fun at the communal pool at our apartment, splashing and playing with pool noodles.

I never had to ask myself what my goal was from week to week. Perhaps this was the flip side of my enormous sense of responsibility. Each day and each week I knew I was accomplishing something important, keeping the boys well and safe and growing.

Reinventing myself as a single woman after fifteen years of marriage had its hilarious moments. The first time I found myself alone in a car with a male driving — it wasn't a date, just a drive to a social event — I was so paralyzed by the strangeness of it that I could hardly talk. I sat there looking over at the guy in the driver's seat, amazed that he wasn't John. He probably thought I was quite strange. I was.

This incident brought home to me how fully my life and identity had been wrapped up in being married. The thought shocked me as, throughout our marriage, I had kept my own name and separate work identity, and generally saw myself as less merged into marriage than many other women. Even with some of my own identity as a starting point, it took a year before I really accepted, inside, that I was single. Until then, every time I told someone I was separated, my eyes filled with tears.

Having left my job in the spring to heal, I waited until mid-August to start job-hunting. I invited a previous boss to lunch to explore openings in the federal government. To my astonishment, he offered me a job on the spot. I accepted and began one of the most satisfying professional roles of my career.

Our living accommodations didn't sort out as easily as my new job. It had been fifteen years since I had lived in a small apartment, and I now had to come to terms with being less financially secure than before. When I invited friends over for a party, I found my pride resistant to having people see our new, sparsely furnished apartment. A part of me felt ashamed that, at age forty-one, I was back in student digs. But I thought *too bad!* This is where the new start has taken me. If they're real friends, they won't care. And they didn't, as far as I could tell. This small victory step was fun.

In telling this, I am embarrassed at how much of my attention was on myself. I tried to watch the boys, to make sure their marks weren't slipping and they were going to their soccer games and hockey practices. But for the first year, I was in survival mode, learning to accept my new realities and cope. I didn't have a lot of energy for David and Steven. I wish now I had been able to focus more on them and take in what they were experiencing and what they needed.

My anger at John didn't fade fast. My stomach tightened and my mouth tensed when upcoming holidays required us to sort out the boys' schedule. I tried hard not to let anger show around the boys. Instead, my strategy was to be neutral. I avoided asking the boys about their father so my feelings wouldn't influence their relationship with him. I believed this was working until one day I started to say, "When you are with me here ..." and David finished my sentence: "It's like Dad doesn't exist." I was floored! Clearly I had gone overboard. I started to acknowledge their dad more in conversations with the boys.

Hanging In for the Long Term

The boys missed us not being a family. A year after the separation, for his birthday dinner for the four of us, David chose Perkins Family Restaurant. When we asked him why he chose that place, he kept saying, "Perkins *Family* Restaurant, I like it." I felt a pang of sadness. Yes, that's where we went for dinner.

Moving between two homes was a hassle for both boys. They had clothes, and later computers, at both places, but the school work, project items, and sports equipment like soccer shoes always needed to be brought with them. They couldn't remember every time. While they got used to living in two homes, it never became easy.

Our new life had its upsides, too. The three of us took a road trip to visit my brother and sister in British Columbia when the boys were seven and ten. We went so the boys could get to know my family, and so I could reassure myself that being a single parent wasn't going to stop me from doing exciting things.

We had so much fun on this crazy trip. The first day, we drove seventeen hours. When we stopped at midday to explore a mountain stream bed, the boys eagerly clambered on rocks, taking risks to cross the stream and acting goofy. They had never seen mountains before, and I felt joy in showing them these marvels. My family welcomed us warmly, and we filled the days with swimming, eating, and telling stories.

Then, back in Winnipeg, I came to an impasse with John. He couldn't afford to pay me for my share of the house. I couldn't buy a dwelling myself without receiving my half of the house value. I didn't want to resort to mediation or lawyers, yet we were at a stalemate.

After several months of frustration, I wrote to his younger sister with whom I had previously been close and asked her to speak with John about it. She never replied to me directly, but within six weeks he did agree to pay me out and I assumed they had talked. I wasn't surprised at his sister's generosity, but in this new state of being divorced, it was hard to know if it would be okay to reach out to his family. This experience reassured me that John's family was actively supporting us all.

Knowing that John would pay me out allowed me to buy a house and escape our noisy apartment building. I could hardly wait. Our neighbourhood had no starter houses in it, and though I badly wanted to move, my mortgage calculations showed me only menacing numbers. I looked at a few houses and felt paralyzed by the fear of being totally house-poor. I spent several months in limbo. Then my father phoned one day, sounding pleased with himself. "I've had an idea! We're going to *give* you some money to help you buy the house!" I could hardly take it in. We had discussed the possibility of a no-interest loan, but this was a different level of help. I gratefully accepted, and returned to house hunting.

Finding a modest house for sale near John's, I went to the credit union for a mortgage. Even with my parents' help, the mortgage numbers towered over me. I got through the signing of papers and was walking down the sidewalk on Main Street when I suddenly felt a pain in the left side of my chest. I thought, *I'm having a heart attack!* The sharp pain persisted. I sank down on a bench and waited until it eased, watching strangers saunter past obliviously. When the doctor at a nearby walk-in clinic told me kindly that it was probably a cramp in my back muscle due to stress, I felt silly. Clearly, my body was reacting to the burden of my first solo house purchase.

My family's support was crucial. My parents and sister and brother accepted the divorce and never badmouthed John in front of the boys. My brother showed particular skill in asking them about their dad, validating that they had another part of their life that wasn't visible when they were with me. My sister listened with endless patience as I sobbed my hurt and fears. I relaxed gratefully during family visits, held by their warmth and stability, food and music.

Another form of support appeared later, when we had been living near John's house for a couple of years. The backyard of our house was joined to our neighbour's backyard, with no fence to break up the grass. The boys would go out our back door, across our backyard onto the neighbour's yard, and through to the next street. This shortcut reduced the trip from my house to John's house to just two minutes by foot. Then one day, the neighbour began building a tall cedar fence, and as it went up, we could see that this special shortcut would be blocked. We felt sad, but resigned; it was their property, after all.

To our delight, when the fence was completed, we saw that the neighbour had built in a tiny child-sized door just for the boys! This family had taken our unique circumstance into account and gone to extra trouble and expense to help us.

Being able to move from one house to the other quite easily — walking or by bike — helped the boys feel that they hadn't lost either parent, even when they were at the other house. Each boy had a bedroom of his own in both houses, with slightly different things in them. John and I didn't try to create the same rules on everything in both houses, as our values on some things, like toy guns, were different. However, we agreed that the boys needed to be responsible and respect both parents. Only once did Steven march off to his dad's house when he didn't like what I was expecting him to do. I immediately phoned John and explained. John sent Steven right back. That was the end of that. John's siding so clearly with me gave Steven a sense of security, I believe, that his world had one large frame that included our two houses. I so appreciated John's support on that.

I was the one setting up medical and dental visits. My crunch points happened when one of the boys was ill on a weekday they were with me. I felt responsible and alone. When one of them was really sick, I missed being able to sit with their father, hold hands, and agonize together. Instead, I sat staring at the deep blue kitchen wall after the boys were in bed, wondering if I should push for more tests or if I was being a fuss-budget. That mother thing.

At least I could phone John — the other person in the world who would be as concerned as I was — and give him news and talk over next steps. The scariest time, when it seemed that Steven might have a brain tumour, John and I both took him to the hospital and stood with him as he underwent an MRI. I was beyond terrified, watching his eighty-pound body disappear into the roaring metal tunnel. Both of us being there eased Steven's fears somewhat, I believe, and we drew comfort from each other's presence. There was no tumour, thank heavens.

More common were school days when the boys were with me and one of them had the flu. I needed to be at work and had no extended family to step in. My stomach clenched when I saw a flushed, unhappy face. I hoped the illness wouldn't last, feeling selfish to be concerned about my work. My office colleagues were supportive but expected me to manage so that nothing impinged on work. One Tuesday morning, a team-building meeting I was facilitating was scheduled to begin shortly. Steven woke pale and feverish. I reluctantly called the team's manager and told her we would need to reschedule. While I respected her as a compassionate person and a great manager, she seemed disappointed that I would make this choice. But the boys' health came first.

The biggest counterweight to the stresses of our new life was having time to myself. The boys were with me from Tuesday after school to Saturday afternoon and with John from Saturday suppertime to Tuesday morning. My free Sunday was gold. I needed time to be quiet, let the excitements and pressures around me settle, and recover my peace. If the rest of the week overflowed with work and grocery shopping and being with the boys and errands and housework, I knew that on Sunday I would have time. Time to sink into the bathtub with a book, go for a walk, and catch up with myself. This need for "me" time wasn't unique. "You mean you have *all Sunday* to yourself?" one friend exclaimed enviously. When I took the boys to music lessons on Saturday mornings, I felt as frazzled as an old straw broom, ends sticking out in all directions. But I knew Sunday was coming.

Our schedule meant I could explore my new identity as a half-time single parent. I felt so uncertain of myself, single after fifteen years of marriage. What would dating be like? Would men still find me attractive? When I entered a new relationship, there was a tingle of possibility that my life as a woman wasn't over even though my marriage had ended. At forty-one, that was exhilarating.

Most of the time, David and Steven had exuberant, relentless energy. When the three of us were together, I often felt like a referee, as they had different temperaments and fought regularly. It was wearing to keep trying to sort out who started it, who was the culprit this time. I didn't worry about this normal sibling tension, but it was hard to enjoy our time together as much as I would have liked. Things improved as they grew older, but somehow I felt that if we had remained an intact family, there might have been more opportunity to spend time with each of them individually.

They loved Christmas morning, when the four of us gathered for breakfast and opening gifts. Some tension between John and me didn't dampen their enjoyment of us all being together. For Christmas dinner they joined their dad's lively and outgoing family. Summer holidays always included time at my family's cottage, with a beach and lots of cousins. The boys learned about both their French and Icelandic heritages.

My Growth

After the first year, I sensed that the crucible of divorce was forging new strength in me. I was reaching deeper inside than ever before, learning to accept my new realities and take action. It felt good to know I could meet the financial responsibilities for myself and the boys, make new friends, and just plain survive. I felt a new pride in my own resilience. I also felt more open. In grieving the end of the marriage, I realized I didn't have all the answers to how to live my life. As the pain subsided, my freedom grew. I felt okay with saying, "I don't know." I got over my reluctance to ask for help; there were lots of things, like sump pumps, I needed to learn about.

Some specific actions helped me. I meditated twenty minutes almost every morning. On any day I skipped this, I would lose my temper faster and snap at the boys. Exercise fuelled me. Getting to workouts wasn't easy, but I had more bounce in my step after leaving the gym.

I learned about seeing gaps and reaching out for ways to fill them. When I first realized my marriage was disintegrating, I thought about my friends nearby. I doubted that my local friendship base was strong enough to support me. I had never been good at developing friendships with other parents as we hung around at hockey and soccer games. I didn't know how to sink into the easy conversations and joking that happened around me.

So I signed up for a facilitated support group with six other women who were also in transition. That group kept me afloat for several years. At weekly meetings we listened, learned from each other, and honoured each others' courage in the journey. Hearing others' struggles showed me I had company, and my problems, while real, weren't as drastic as those others had experienced. I learned unexpected things. Once, we were using markers to draw, and I realized I had chosen brown — shit-brown, actually — to fill in a picture. I laughed. My feelings emerged in unforeseen ways.

With time, the group support, and periodic solo counselling, I gradually was able to consider my part in our marriage problems. I saw my reluctance to look straight at things that might disturb me, whether others' actions or my own. I saw that I loved to be right. Oh, and that there was a part of me that would like to control the whole world. (Still working on that, I am informed by reliable sources.) This self-knowledge wasn't comfortable at first, yet it freed me from feeling like a helpless victim and deepened my sense of connection with others.

Except for Sunday afternoons, I didn't feel relaxed for years. I was always alert to what else might be coming, what else needed to be done. I also missed, and know the boys did too, a sense of continuity from when they were little — one family growing together through the years. This still gives me an occasional pang of regret.

After the first two years, my relationship with John softened. One of us would have the boys for Christmas Eve, and on Christmas morning the other parent would come over to open gifts and have a Christmas brunch. John and I even exchanged small gifts, though gingerly. My anger ebbed away. He appeared to be getting on with his life, continuing his relationship with the woman he was seeing after we separated.

I had one seven-year romantic relationship, and then three years later married Bruce; we have now been married ten years. Perhaps I will never know how to be in a relationship that is easy, but Bruce and I let each other into our realities and share a precious grounding of trust and love. We hold hands, and he makes me laugh. John now seems like a brother with whom I am no longer close.

What Co-Parenting Meant

Our co-parenting meant that the boys spent time with both their dad and me every week, and maintained a solid, genuine relationship with us both. They had fun on holidays with each of us. They were able to stay in the same neighbourhood they had grown up in, with the same friends, bus routes, and schools, which gave them stability. Their friends were welcome at both houses. They shared travel, family, and interests with both of us.

I wanted to raise our boys so they would realize most fully who they could be. I passionately didn't want the divorce, in which they had no responsibility or choice, to hurt their chances of growing up successfully.

Did we achieve this goal? Both boys continued to do all right in school, though their marks dropped a bit in the first years. In pictures taken at that time, they both look uncertain — doing okay but not feeling secure. The best I can say about the early years is that the boys survived and didn't fall into obvious dysfunction.

It wasn't until each boy hit high school that I started to feel that they were doing fine, finding their way as all adolescents must. Their choice of friends and how they dealt with those around them, including their dad and me, showed they had good values and were starting to get it together as young adults. My worry about the impacts of the divorce didn't end then, but it subsided.

Now they are engaging, well-rounded men. They both have developed their interests into livelihoods, and sustain friendships and relationships. Sometimes I wonder if the uncertainty from the divorce deterred them from experimenting on the edge — for example, with drugs — since they already felt their world was less than fully secure. But there is no way of knowing if this is true.

Overall, I believe that co-parenting benefited the boys greatly. They have strong relationships with both John and me. They didn't have to deal with either of us being the bad guy, and they didn't have to choose a side. I rejoice at the bond I have with each of them; it feels closer and more authentic than the relationship I had with my own parents. Both sons have told John and me how much they value us. There is no sweeter thing to hear.

Each step on my journey changed me. Finding the courage to leave the marriage connected me to my own strength. Developing a way to co-parent gave me confidence to be less conventional than before; being eccentric was freeing. My growth helped me hold the children's interests high and also meet my own needs. This has helped me in other relationships — romantic, social, and career. And of course, I am a work-in-progress.

Those first months and years felt overwhelming. I would like to be able to go back now and reassure that years-ago-Karen. I would say, "It will be okay. The boys are going to be fine, and so will you. Pay attention to everything, including your feelings and the boys', and don't hesitate to seek support. Trust yourself. You are a strong woman and you will grow stronger. All will be well."

I co-parented the only way I could figure out to do it. It didn't occur to me that others might do it another way. The first thing I learned from these interviews was how many different co-parenting journeys exist, each complex and multi-faceted.

Because each parent could provide their story only from their perspective, you may, like me, long to hear from the other partner or from the children. How did it feel to them? How were they impacted? That information wasn't available; with every story, we can only receive what was offered and know it is partial.

Sometimes I had trouble understanding the choices that parents made. As you read the stories, you may react with "She shouldn't have done that!" Or "He should have done it differently." Or "I would do it differently." Please remember: parenting is very personal. We don't have to agree with the choices parents made in order to learn from their thoughts and feelings and how their decisions played out.

The stories that follow are abbreviated. At the core of every one lies the parent's determination to make things work for their children.

2 Health, Self-Management, and Many Ways to Share

Do what you can, with what you have, where you are.
— THEODORE ROOSEVELT

Starting these interviews, I believed that each parent's main task would be to get over the upheaval of divorce, find a new balance of parenting with kids living in two homes, and carry on. I pictured moms and dads travelling a path, starting from the two-parent-family world and settling into the co-parenting world in a place that felt comfortable or at least workable.

It turns out it's not that simple. In the new world of co-parenting, there is no single model and many choices to make in constructing a new life. Co-parenting is accomplished via many different paths.

You can create a way that works for your situation. You must discover and build your own path — no one else's solutions will fit perfectly for you. I found my own answers. So can you. To choose your way forward, you'll need to step back and get some perspective.

Seeing the Big Picture

As parents, it can be hard to detach from strong feelings and see how you fit into a broader perspective. But to build a new life successfully, you must see the big picture. When you can do this, you're no longer right in the middle — or muddle. You understand your situation a bit differently and discover new choices.

A pattern emerged from the many interviews, which offered a way to understand how families operate. Each parent's story contained the same elements: the building blocks of families. The blocks, or elements, looked different in each story and combined differently for everyone, but once I recognized the elements as important, I could see the big picture of families. Bear with me and you'll gain a new way to understand families, including your own.

The main elements of a family are the parents and the children:

- the physical, mental, and financial health of each parent
- the ages and physical and mental health of the children

Taken together, these elements not only describe each family but also define the choices for co-parenting. Each element allows for some things to happen, and requires actions, as well. Let's look at some definitions:

1. **Physical health**
   This is often taken for granted. What is your level of physical health? Can you walk, sit, climb, and lift things without stress or pain? Can you drive a car or use the subway system? Do you require medications or special supports? When physical health is lacking, low energy can make everyday parenting hard and keep parents from being alert and involved. Sick kids need extra care and energy from their families.

2. **Mental health**
   This is your ability to function day to day both as a competent adult and a person who maintains connections with others. This usually suffers for a while after divorce. Most folks go through a period of anxiety and upheaval but recover with time and support. Conditions such as depression, which may occur intermittently or persist for years, make parenting harder.

3. **Financial health**
   This is your ability to make or access money. Low income may force a parent to take a job at a distance from the other parent. Debts or scarcity add extra stress to daily living and may add

tension to negotiations between parents. Families with a child or parent with special needs often face extra living costs.

With good physical, mental, and financial health in both parents, you can likely find many ways to co-parent that will work. You can meet the children's needs in various combinations of care and living arrangements. It still won't be easy at first, because you'll feel hurt, sad, or angry. But you will have choices.

Extra needs from any aspect of health, either the parents' or children's, put more demands on the whole system. As Chapter 6, "Co-Parenting with Mental Health Conditions," and Chapter 7, "Co-Parenting Children with Special Needs," illustrate, those demands can be not only large but also overwhelming.

To better see your own big picture and others', take a few minutes for the following exercise.

To Sharpen and Expand Your Perspective

At the moment, you see everything from where you are standing, as we all do. Now pull an imaginary camera lens up and back, as if you are standing on a big hill looking down at your situation. Jot down how you see *your* situation.

Start by looking at health. What is the condition of

- your physical and mental health;
- your ex-partner's physical and mental health;
- your children's physical and mental health;
- your financial health; and
- your ex-partner's financial health?

Writing down those answers is a good start to sharpening your perspective. But there's more.

How We Handle What We've Got

The physical and mental health of parents and children and the financial health of parents cover a lot of ground. When it's time to work out how you will actually co-parent after divorce, two other factors show up neon-bright. Both will impact how you deal with your health factors and your ex-partner: expectations of co-parenting and self-management skills.

Expectations include how you see your role and your ex-partner's role in your co-parenting after divorce. Do you imagine a fifty-fifty time split? Weekends only? Little communication, or daily updates? No financial support, or lots? As the stories show, what parents wanted to do seemed to depend on their past experiences — in their own lives or the lives of family or close friends. If both parents had similar expectations, negotiations could be short and easy. If expectations varied greatly? Long and messy.

Each parent needs to have a number of **self-management skills**:

1. **Emotional awareness**
    This is the ability to see how your own feelings and actions are impacting those around you. We all know people who are oblivious to the emotional wake they leave behind them, who never see the hurt looks or rolling of eyes as they walk away. People with a low level of emotional awareness drift past others' hurt or anger, not connecting it with anything they have said or done.

2. **Ability to accept reality**
    With this skill, you are not stuck in the past, still needing it to be different. You use your energy for responding to what's happening now. You seldom use the phrase, "If only ...," focusing instead on the present and the future.

3. **Dependability**
    You can be counted on to do what you promised to do, usually. If you break a promise, you acknowledge it and make amends where you can. This predictable behaviour allows adults and children to trust you.

4. **Ability to take others' needs and welfare into account, especially children's**
    You pay attention to others' situations; your actions reflect more than your own needs and interests.

5. **Ability to control yourself so that you don't abuse others**
   This includes both words and actions; a vicious or careless slur can cause damage for years.

This may seem obvious, but it's important enough to say anyway: the level of self-management of each mother and father makes a big difference in how they parent — together or apart.

Self-management skills usually stay fairly level in adults. However, they may shift with significant life events or learning experiences. Getting divorced, for instance, can teach new levels of self-control or awareness. Individual or group counselling, coaching, journaling, and reading can increase self-management skills. Other experiences can lower skill levels. Substance abuse may decrease a person's level of self-management for a period of time. A parent in the grip of alcohol may do a poor job of taking others' needs into account.

Many parents have high levels of all of these self-management skills; others have medium or high levels in some of them, but not all. Some parents have very low skills.

> For another way of considering your own readiness to move forward with co-parenting, see the questions in **Appendix 2.**

If you are like me, when reading the list of self-management skills, you find it easy to look at your ex-partner and make judgments. Fair enough. We need to look hard at ourselves, though, too, and ask, "What is *my* level of self-management right now?"

You have already noted your health factors for yourself, ex-partner, and children. Now, you need to also detail the expectations of you and your partner:

- What are *your* expectations of co-parenting?
- What are *your* self-management skills?
- What are your *ex-partner's* expectations of co-parenting?
- What are *their* self-management skills?

It may take some time for you to pull back enough to make these assessments.

When you have made your notes, sit with them for a few minutes. What do you notice? How do you feel as you look at each part? At the whole picture? What are the positives? It's easy to overlook what's good as your attention is snagged by the weak areas.

Why is this important? What difference does it make?

Expectations and self-management skills are worth looking at because they help explain why parenting negotiations flow smoothly or hit big snags. If you see that you and your ex have wildly different expectations of how you will co-parent, it makes sense that your negotiations on co-parenting will be long and hard.

Thinking, "We're having all these problems because he/she is such a jerk!" doesn't get you very far, whether it's true or not. In fact, it can mire you in endless blaming. You need a wider, more objective view, and these questions help you find it.

Once you see more of the big picture, two things can happen. First, it may be easier to *accept your reality* as it is right now. This is a key self-management skill. It's hard enough to deal with an ex-partner who has expectations different than your own. Say you feel that sending your kids to a summer sports camp is a no-brainer — *such* an important thing — but your ex sees it as an unnecessary expense. Spending time stewing in frustration, thinking, "But she shouldn't see it that way!" makes your life harder. Accepting the reality, for the moment, that your ex has a different view than yours eases that endless gut-churning feeling. Then you can relax a bit and start searching for options and ways to move forward.*

Second, it gives you a chance to look at your situation and ask, "What is within my control?" This can be a tough question to answer. Often you won't like the answer you get, because, failing legal involvement, it usually comes back: *yourself*. I know that's not the answer I wanted. But hey, if it's hard to influence a partner while you are married, why would it be any easier when you're not married? Understanding and accepting

---

*Accepting your ex-partner as they are doesn't mean accepting abusive behaviour. It means letting go of needing to change their view of the world.

exactly what you can control is like eating a protein-rich meal. You are prepared for sustained, powerful action.

Let's put it all together. Looking at your own situation, you have assessed the big picture:

- health of parents and children
- parents' expectations
- parents' self-management skills

Are you ready for some examples? Many of these stories include parents struggling to see and accept what was within their control, and gradually finding answers. Their attempts to control their partner's behaviours, especially with the children, changed as they understood what worked and what didn't.

As you read the stories, watch how each parent's health, expectations, and self-management skills showed up in how they made decisions and carried them out. Notice your own reactions to what parents did and didn't do, and how you are the same as or different from them. Remember that we each have to start from where we are, which may be a place where our skills are low and our options, limited.

ZACK'S AND VIVIAN'S STORIES: DIVORCING WITH KINDNESS, SLOWLY

special needs child • lesbian relationship
postponement of separation

"There was no literature to follow. We were making it up as we went along, trying to keep the focus on the kids," said Zack, a fifty-four-year-old college professor. He and his wife, Vivian, celebrated their twentieth wedding anniversary, then agreed to divorce. They had been divorced one year, co-parenting a sixteen-year-old daughter and an eighteen-year-old son, when I interviewed them. Both Zack and Vivian were willing to talk with me, separately.

Zack sounded calm and almost philosophical, but admitted that at first he had had a very hard time keeping friendly relations. "I pushed down my own feelings of hurt and anger to make the best of it and keep the kids first."

Zack's and Vivian's different communication styles had caused friction between them for years. Then Vivian realized she wanted to be in a lesbian relationship. Zack rolled with the punches. "Our relationship changed as she came to realizations about herself. I tried to be supportive of her because she's a friend."

Zack accepted the reality that his long-held vision of the future wouldn't work. At fifty-four years old, he found he had to make a new plan. He and Vivian were still friends, with twenty years of shared history between them, but the road ahead was diverging. Vivian, forty-nine, had worked as an office manager for many years. Her voice sounded light and clear as she described not only changing plans but shifting to a whole new life direction. "Letting go of the dream of husband and house and family with kids has been a roller coaster of joy and fear. I'm still scared on a daily basis. He makes more money than me, and I have fleeting fears I will end up living in a cardboard box."

Vivian hadn't begun counselling with divorce in mind. The pair started with marriage therapy, but both had changed so much it wasn't working. Vivian went to a different therapist and realized she wanted a divorce. Then Zack and Vivian found a counsellor to help them divorce with kindness and minimize disruptions for the kids.

Planning Around Parenting

Deciding to separate was only the first step. How to do it? They discussed moving into separate dwellings and reluctantly concluded they couldn't afford it. They considered taking turns living in the family home, and realized that neither of them wanted to be raising two teenagers alone.

Each valued the other's support. Their sixteen-year-old daughter, Joyce, had significant special needs, both academically and behaviourally. She needed a lot of parenting, still, to help with home-work, and to set clear limits and rewards for her. Zack and Vivian's unease about parenting alone caused them to pause and seek another option that would work for them and their children. Both had high self-management skills, which allowed them to consider various ways they could work together.

After considerable discussion, they decided to keep sharing the house, and parenting, for at least one more year. Then their son, Nathan, would graduate and begin studying at university.

Going from being married and sharing a home to being divorced in the same home took much discussion and care. They began hold-ing regular family meetings to keep everyone up to date with changes. "We have had to redefine roles, which meant more communicating than before," said Zack. "I now take the role of day-to-day organizing. Nathan is very social, he wants to go out with friends a lot, he needs supervision. We also talk money. Two teenagers can be pretty darned expensive! We've encouraged the kids to help with costs."

Before, Vivian had been the more involved parent and homemaker. Hiring a housekeeper freed time for them both and removed a source of friction. They also set a new parenting strategy, seeing that Joyce was now taking direction better from Zack than from Vivian. Vivian pulled back from her highly active parenting style, knowing that Zack was stepping forward with his own approach. She sighed. "What's hard for me is letting go. Joyce may fail this year. Till now, on Sundays I took away all distractions, like her phone, and she didn't get it back until Friday when the teachers signed off on her work. Now Zack will take over, and I'll support him."

Both Zack and Vivian struggled to choose the best way to parent Joyce as she grew and changed, while they were working through their own life shifts. They jointly decided that when they sold the house and lived separately, Joyce would live with her dad. Zack acknowledged there would be challenges, as he knew Joyce could be negative and moody. It would be different. "I told her, 'I'm your best buddy. You piss me off, you've got nobody.' I let her know she had to step up and take re-sponsibility for her actions."

Although the parents discussed their situation openly with their children, both saw that staying in the same house was allowing their kids to ignore their parents' divorce. Both parents seemed content to let the children take their time acknowledging and accepting the changes.

"Their heads are firmly buried in the sand," said Vivian. "Nathan just acknowledged that we're selling the house. Joyce has told her friends, 'My mom said she's gonna kick me out.'"

Zack commented, "Next year, when we sell the house and move, all this will emerge."

Proportional Cost Sharing

Each parent had a bank account, plus a shared house account to which Zack contributed 60 percent, Vivian, 40. Zack sounded more comfortable with the financial arrangements than some of the other fathers interviewed. He believed that he should contribute more to the joint account than Vivian as his earnings were greater. Yet he did worry about being able to recover financially from the divorce before he retired. He and Vivian had timed their divorce partly to allow them each to establish a financial base while they were still earning income.

Their Journeys

Both parents were dating. Zack explained, "We're keeping that outside of the house, for now. We coordinate schedules, like roommates. We let each other know when we're going out. I want to get out, listen to music, go dancing."

Zack felt reluctant to let his friends know what was happening until the divorce was done, telling people on a need-to-know basis. This meant that few friends were aware he could use support. He saw a therapist instead, intermittently, for eight months. "He was great, so supportive. He suggested books, kept me on track, and helped me to see how this could work."

Vivian reached out to close friends, her therapist, and her new lesbian community for support. "I always thought I did a better job at parenting because I paid more attention. I'm realizing now that we parent differently, and we don't have to parent the same. I've learned to communicate better.

I've realized the importance of slowing down, creating relationships, and being in the moment. I'm more confident. I've come into my own."

Both parents knew they were still in the middle of their transition. Said Vivian, "We're getting rid of the bad aspects of the relationship and keeping what's positive. I'm kind of proud of us."

Even with physical health and relative financial health, this was a difficult separation. Two factors added complexity. The first was Vivian's discovery of her lesbian orientation. Every family member needed to get used to her changed identity.

The second factor, Joyce's special needs, made parenting more complicated, especially with her growing emotional distance from her mother. Both Zack and Vivian worried about how Joyce would fare with the shift from Vivian's approach to Zack's less hands-on style. As parents, we only know what works by trying it, and Zack had resolved to step up to the full parenting role with Joyce, adapting as needed.

Zack's and Vivian's shared expectations of parenting formed a base for planning. Their deliberate decision-making led them to cohabit in their house for a year, and then have Joyce live with her father. Their high self-management skills allowed them to discuss and accept their new realities and build a unique path forward. They both were able to grow into a different way of parenting and find ways to make their new arrangements work. I was touched by their courage.

Zack and Vivian put a premium on living close to each other. That isn't always true, or possible, as the next story shows.

STEFAN'S STORY:
LONG-DISTANCE PARENTING

decision-making • influence of early family templates
parenting from a distance

Stefan and his wife, Georgia, separated when their son, Ben, was four. Stefan was twenty-eight, Georgia, twenty-four. They were living on the outskirts of a university town in Kansas while Stefan finished his Ph.D. in social work. A man used to looking at his own behaviour, Stefan seemed to be sorting as he told me his story: this worked, that didn't.

Regret shaded Stefan's voice as he reflected on the influence of his own family history on his choices as a dad. His parents divorced when he was small, and his father maintained a polite relationship with him, but from a distance. Even when they were adults, living only half a mile apart, father and son saw each other just twice a year. Stefan's mother, in his words "a difficult person," tried to be supportive of Stefan and his choices, but she lived in Boston and her regular visits to Kansas weren't enough for Stefan to feel close to her. His template for family contained a pattern of geographic spaces between people, which he brought with him into his own marriage.

Stefan left his marriage to escape Georgia's anger, which he found toxic. "She threatened to kill herself. I didn't think I could make it work, but I wish I hadn't succumbed to my need to get away from that intensity, that anger."

Soon after separating from Georgia, Stefan began a long-distance relationship with a woman in Chicago. After two years, he moved to Chicago, more to get away from Georgia than to strengthen his new relationship. His move began his long-distance parenting of Ben, which lasted twelve years.

Georgia raged at Stefan when he told her he was moving away, skeptical that Stefan would stay involved with Ben. Over time, however, she mellowed. She saw his sustained fathering actions, and came to trust Stefan more.

Making Long-Distance Parenting Work

Twice a month, Stefan would spend a three-day weekend with Ben. They would alternate flying. On one visit, Stefan would fly to Kansas to see Ben; for the next visit, Ben would fly to Chicago. Stefan volunteered at Ben's school, supporting the teacher in the classroom every Friday of his visits to Kansas. There, he could not only interact with Ben but also see how Ben was getting along with his classmates, and get to know them, too.

These trips required determination, money, and support. To pay for all the flights, and to afford child support, Stefan worked two jobs. An old friend in Kansas let him stay in her house during his monthly visits. "Friends with kids would loan me their car and take me to the airport. Only my friends' support made all this possible." His mother and sister always encouraged him to keep on making this choice work, knowing its importance to Ben and to Stefan.

"The hardest part of each month was the end of those weekends," Stefan said, remembering. "I was either getting on a plane or putting Ben on a plane. It felt brutal. Ben felt close to me, he knew that I cared. But he was also sad, as if another relationship took precedence over him."

Six years prior to my interview with him, Stefan began a new relationship, and he now has a daughter with his new partner. His bond with his five-year-old daughter has been different than his connection with Ben. "It's more everyday; it feels more complete. Ben knows I love him, and I was a consistent, frequent presence in his life. Those three or four days, I constructed my world around him. But it's not the same. I would like to have been as involved with my son as I am with my daughter. If I had this to do over again, I would make a different choice."

Once Stefan experienced everyday parenting with family in one place, he realized the cost of his decision to move away. When he felt that he couldn't make things work living near Georgia, moving away had seemed his only choice. Two factors influenced his decision. The first was his family template: Stefan's experience of a distant relationship with his father made parenting from afar seem a natural option. The second factor was his compelling need to escape Georgia's anger. He wasn't able to step back to consider other options for parenting Ben. If he had thought to search, Stefan might have found choices such as parallel parenting.* Or he might have found, through counselling, a way to feel less overpowered by Georgia's anger. Increasing his emotional awareness, part of self-management, may have given him more options.

In several ways, Stefan's choice worked. Through holding two jobs and accepting help from friends, he created ways to be part of Ben's

---

*Some high-conflict couples use this strategy, where both parents have significant time with their child, but the communication between the parents is written, through a detailed parenting plan, emails, and a notebook. See Appendix 3 for resources.

life. Ben had real involvement from Stefan, and a chance to learn from talking with him and doing things together. Georgia, over time, grew to trust Stefan as a father. Both parents evolved and were able to give Ben stability.

Yet in retrospect, after he was able to live everyday parenting with his daughter, Stefan realized how much he had missed with his son. He felt his decision to parent Ben at a distance had cost both of them too much. A painful lesson.

Many factors drive our decisions. In the midst of swirling emotions, taking time to step back and fully weigh our options is hard to do — and essential.

GLORIA'S STORY: DIFFERENT VIEWS OF PARENTING

control struggles • growth
help from the unexpected

When thirty-year-old Gloria and her husband, Fred, split three years before her interview with me, Gloria wanted to co-parent two-year-old Janey. Right after the separation, Gloria had to almost persuade Fred to spend time with Janey; he hadn't wanted to be a dad and wasn't sure he was cut out to be an involved father post-divorce. With differing expectations, the parents took years to find their way. Gloria, a computer technician, impressed me with her sturdy tone: "I don't regret what happened; there's been so much growth. It wasn't the wrong path, just a difficult path."

Gloria liked the idea of co-parenting, because she didn't want to be a single mom and she wanted Janey to grow up knowing her father. Her initial fears about Fred's low involvement faded as Fred's new girlfriend, Anya, seemed to help Fred warm up to fatherhood. "Fred and I weren't good together, but he was a different person with Anya. She was good with Janey, and they seemed to be doing fine." After a few months, Gloria got everyone together to work out the best schedule for Janey. They decided to go week-on/week-off, with no child support.

Although they agreed on timing, it soon became clear that Gloria and Fred saw co-parenting differently. "My ex felt that his parenting was none of my business. He'd say, 'She's at my house, my rules, my diet. When she's at your house, your rules, your diet.' I would say, 'But she's one person!'" Gloria agonized over the differences, anxious and frustrated that Fred wouldn't align his parenting with hers.

This conflict led to intense strain for Gloria during the weeks she didn't have Janey. "For months I would cry and freak out once she had gone with her dad — I felt unsure of who would be caring for her, whose car she would be riding in, what she was eating. It was really tough." Gloria sank into a depression for weeks and once tried to take her own life.

Tension between them led Fred to take Gloria to court. There she got the message that she needed to back off. "We got a parenting plan. I ended up letting go for a while, trying to ride with it. Sometimes my rage would come out by phone or emails at him, but never in front of our daughter. I learned, slowly, to let go."

Within a year of the separation, a fire destroyed Gloria's house and all her possessions. An extra hurdle! To earn more money, she reluctantly moved eighty kilometres from Hope, British Columbia, to Abbotsford, where she had found a better-paying job and could receive family support. The parenting plan for Janey required both parents to give sixty days' notice of moving, but because of the fire, Gloria moved abruptly to Abbotsford, giving only thirty days' notice. Fred thought Gloria was trying to take Janey away from him, and called his lawyer.

Returning to court could have made things worse. Instead, it had a surprising effect, as Fred gained unexpected insights from a judge's comments.

Gloria recalled, "We were both feeling kind of battle-weary by then. Fred told the judge, accusingly, that I had moved away to make more money, to have a better life. The judge started to laugh and asked Fred, 'Are you listening to yourself? That's wonderful that she is doing that for her daughter. She is giving up a lot of time with Janey.'

"I could see a light going on in him. At that moment, it clicked in his head that I wasn't trying to mess anyone up, I was trying to make our life better. Since then, things have been easier; my ex and I are on the same page re: the details of Janey's life."

Gloria felt good about her move to Abbotsford as an interim step, though it was hard having Janey only on weekends. "I felt guilty, like I was a bad parent, like I couldn't meet our daughter's needs. My ex and his girlfriend were providing more than I could — that was how I saw it, for a while."

Growth and Rewards

Surviving the loneliness of separation and the shock of the fire, combined with support from her sister and friends, increased Gloria's self-confidence. "I've gotten stronger and learned to make it on my own."

Writing showed her new insights. "I wrote everything down. At one point I even made a book of our relationship, to get everything in perspective. Blogging on open forums helped; even if no one was listening, it felt like someone was."

She recognized her own contribution to events. "I had to do some soul-searching. I've learned that I have a bad temper, and now I can see how it affects people. My whole life I had been a free spirit, thinking just about myself. This changed my mindset, because it wasn't about me anymore. Now, for Janey, I think ahead. When she starts first grade, I plan to move back to Hope."

Fred also grew. His relationship with his new partner, Anya, changed him from wanting little to do with Janey to taking a big part in her life. As well, the judge's remarks in court offered him a different way to interpret Gloria's actions, which let him trust Gloria more.

Gloria's changed behaviour meant that Fred felt less pressure. When she learned to stop trying to control Janey's life with Fred, he in turn could relax his guard enough to learn from the judge's blunt comments. The relationship between the parents improved, slowly, as they grew in different ways. Janey gained two parents who worked together for her.

Almost five, Janey has benefited from the co-parenting. "She's a cool kid — smart, talented, and creative. What four-year-old says, 'Pleased to meet you!' She is beginning to understand that we are all a huge family and there are lots of ways to be a family. On her fourth birthday, I invited my ex and his wife over for cake and ice cream. Janey looked around and said, 'So many people love me!' I felt good. That's what I was working for."

Anything we learn about ourselves will impact our relationships. It can be freeing to recognize our part in what has happened, as Gloria did, because we feel more powerful and less like victims. Increasing our self-management skills gradually pays off in many directions.

GARY'S STORY:
KEEPING A STRONG FAMILY CIRCLE

redefining separation
postponement of full, new relationships

Gary looked just like you want a contractor to be: alert and dependable. He and his wife, Anna, friends from age sixteen, had been married twenty-five years at our interview. Their daughters were then twenty-five and twenty-seven.

Early in this chapter, we saw how Zack and Vivian's shared picture of post-split living helped them. Gary and Anna both held the same, unusually strong expectation of family stability. They believed that, having had children, they both had a commitment to those children until they turned eighteen. Gary said, "Once you have a family, that's it. You have a family, and you can't just leave that one and wander off and start another one." Their self-management skills helped them sustain their family pact.

Twelve years before I interviewed him, both parents had felt their paths diverging, as Anna dived deep into graduate studies and Gary focused on building his business. They wanted to spend their time differently, which led to stress and arguments. They decided to separate but not divorce, and to keep every other aspect of family as it had been.

Gary's lawyer helped them to set up a separation agreement with little conflict. Gary moved into a nearby condo and the parents set up bedrooms for their girls, thirteen and fifteen, in both homes. Gary and Anna agreed not to introduce other mates or partners into the family until the children were grown. They maintained this intact family circle for ten years.

Separated and Still a Family

In order to maintain the children's feeling of the family connection both parents attended all family events. Gary and Anna co-operated fully to fill in when one of them was travelling. Each parent had had a separate bank account all along, plus a shared family account; they treated the acquisition of a second home as a required investment. They kept any romantic connections out of sight so that complications, such as step-siblings or extended family, would not strain the girls.

"We had tremendous support from our immediate family and parents," Gary told me. "They could see that we were taking a bold new approach to support the children, and we had many positive comments."

The co-responsibility for the children was paramount. Any other relationships by either parent were very discreet, so as not to complicate the core family circle. In fact, Gary and Anna both delayed forming full, new sexual relationships for ten years in order to preserve the family for their children. They therefore avoided becoming part of any other family. Any sense of sacrifice Gary may have felt was outweighed by his sense of fulfillment from preserving the family. Not many parents are prepared to postpone developing full, new relationships for ten years, but it seemed to work for Gary and Anna. It is a bold alternative worth considering.

Gary felt their approach paid off. "The respect from our children increased. They got to see who I really was, and who their mom really was."

In the two years before our interview, the pact had been dissolving, as the daughters were now adults starting their own families. Gary felt great pride in the stability and psychological safety that he and Anna had provided. "We should have another category, besides separated and divorced, to leave more room for parents to take social responsibility for their families."

JOE'S AND SANDY'S STORIES:
LIVING APART, LIVING TOGETHER

learning to be a divorced dad • lesbian relationship
a new living solution

Growth, determination, and flexibility helped Joe and Sandy create a novel co-parenting arrangement. They wanted to co-parent when they split, but struggled to make it work. Joe, a soft-spoken teacher, had married Sandy, an actress and playwright, when they were in their late twenties. Now in their forties, both agreed to be interviewed, offering their differing perspectives over time.

Sandy felt they were both young emotionally when they married. "It was challenging from the get-go." After their first child was born, the conflict between them grew. The marriage wasn't working, but they couldn't afford two houses, so they stayed together. They separated and reunited several more times until they split permanently, after twelve years. They had children who were then three, six, and nine.

Early Stage Adjustments

To manage the costs of two households, they bought a nearby duplex and tried living side by side. Hostilities flared so often, however, that after a year Joe moved out. For several years Sandy stayed in the duplex while Joe took small lodgings nearby. At first he had two rooms, and then found an apartment with a yard.

Sandy struggled with guilt and feeling unfairly blamed. "Joe kept viewing this as a temporary situation and wouldn't get serious about finding permanent lodgings. The community didn't understand why I wouldn't let him come back. He looked like a wonderful man to outsiders, and they saw me angry and crying. It was hard to be the bad guy. I thought that if I could just be more patient and open-minded, this would all work."

As with Stefan earlier in this chapter, Joe's history influenced his view of family and divorce. "My parents divorced when I was young; my mom remarried and my stepdad adopted me. To me, he was my dad. My own dad wasn't around much, and when we split, I felt I was becoming my dad — that guy who moves out and loses touch with the kids. I had no picture of what a successful divorced dad looked like."

Joe needed to accept the separation and build a new belief in himself as a divorced father.

At first, he felt threatened at any unequal time split with the children. "I was so used to seeing the kids every day. They went back and forth nearly every night. It was wearing them out! If I didn't fight for equal time, I felt I was failing as a dad. Then I let that go and realized I could be an effective parent no matter what."

Joe began building a new picture of how to be a dad from his room in a big Victorian house. "The first time the kids were with me, they were sick and I didn't have a thermometer, Tylenol, none of that. I had to go out and get it. That was a big growing thing for me — becoming a nurturing guy, not only a fix-it guy, making sure they had meals, taking on roles I wasn't accustomed to."

Joe grew inside first, coming to believe he could be a good dad post-divorce. Then he developed new skills on the outside so he could take on a full parenting role.

He continued to grieve the lost relationship, but learned to take the children places without Sandy. "It felt like rubbing salt into the wound to be with them and not her."

Sandy struggled in different ways. "While co-parenting was a given, I wasn't clear on how it would happen. I felt so angry, I wanted nothing to do with him. When I realized I could divorce him but would still need to see him because of the kids, it felt like a death sentence. I felt physically ill."

Sandy entered a lesbian relationship. Beyond the many questions it raised for her personally, it also complicated planning the divorce. "Would he use the same-sex relationship in the courts? What were my rights?" Her fears subsided only when the divorce went through smoothly.

Growing into Co-Parenting

Joe saw a counsellor who showed him patterns from his family of origin and helped him build self-awareness. He also joined a meditation group and spent time in nature whenever he could, slowly letting go of the past. "I've learned more patience with life and with myself. I go a little slower now on the inside. I like that I've learned to not just say what's on the tip of my tongue. Now I pay attention to what's happening for others. Not saying stuff can be as important as saying stuff."

A new relationship offered Joe a model of parenting post-divorce. He started dating a woman who was seven years out of a divorce, with a daughter and an ex who was an involved dad. Joe saw them both chaperoning a school camping trip, and noted how well it worked as they talked together and interacted.

His girlfriend's perspective gave Joe new insights. "As a single mom, she pointed out that no one was getting rich. I could see her frustrations in being on her own and trying to raise her child the best she could. I could talk to her about my divorce and I wouldn't always get sympathy.

"Sometimes she'd say, 'You've got to look at it from this point of view — Sandy's afraid right now.' I wouldn't have even considered it. It helped me."

Joe's broader perspective of family turned down the heat of friction with Sandy.

Leaving the marriage sparked Sandy's growth. "When I married, I chose to stop evolving. I blamed Joe for so long. Now there was no one to blame but me. I had to let all my questions about our marriage go and figure out: Who am I? How can I take care of me and the kids? I wanted so much to do the right things, but there were no hard and fast rules, no way to know what was best." Support from her family and friends, as well as her new partner, sustained her. "My best friends kept saying, 'Get some boundaries!'"

Sandy learned new self-management skills, seeing how she impacted those around her. "I tended to choose things for others. I've learned I need to ask before I do something." She also grew in confidence by tackling hard things. When she heard a sound downstairs, there was no one else to wake up and go check it out. She did it herself, and felt empowered.

A Different Solution

Joe's work began to take him four days at a time to a nearby city, every two weeks. He kept his apartment as his home base and found makeshift lodgings in the new city. After a few months, the stress and confusion were wearing him out. He would wake up not knowing where he was, not having what he needed with him. Living in two places showed him what his kids were experiencing.

He turned a corner. "I started really listening to what the kids were saying and to the possibility of doing something different." He began to consider how it might work to share a single dwelling.

Three years post-separation, Joe and Sandy agreed to share a house together. Joe, Sandy, and her partner, Sherri, moved in with the three children. This move eased financial stress, as Joe had been paying child support plus rent. The children gained a unified home base, which they loved, but it made new demands on the adults.

Okay, "new demands on the adults" is an understatement. For a divorced mother and father to share a house with a new partner, same-sex or not, takes a lot of effort, communication, and self-management. Sandy said, "The children really like not having to go back and forth! They asked very intelligent questions when we were planning the new house. We do week-on/week-off as parents now; it gives good continuity. If you're on, you are the duty parent and handle meals and transportation. There are lots of parents on hand for extras, like throwing a ball or helping with homework. I appreciate the times when I am not the parent on duty, so I can have a phone call without someone bursting in to sit on my lap."

As in any group of three, sometimes two paired up against one. The pair, and the one left over, shifted often. The children joined the dynamic flow. If the adults began to argue, the kids would tackle whoever was making the attack, to protect the other. Conflicts arose about finances and bedtimes, as in any family. They held a family meeting each week to discuss anything upcoming or contentious, and the adults used mediation when needed.

Impacts on the Adults

Sandy found it challenging to find time to spend with her new partner. "Yet I think we have more time than most married couples have! My new relationship with Joe is as liberating as I thought it would be. Now I like our relationship. We can look at what we *can* be together. We don't see our split as a failure now."

Joe: "We have a beautiful home, and I feel pride. We wouldn't have had this otherwise. We go on family vacations, hide Easter eggs, go to games and track meets. I don't think we would have worked so hard on ourselves if we had stayed married. We are more intentional as parents, as working housemates, than ever before."

Impacts on the Children

Joe saw the kids reaping huge benefits. "They have always known we both love them. Now they can feel safe and relax, knowing that things aren't going to blow up. They were inhibited about telling me about things they did when they were with Sandy, until I reached out and invited Sherri to breakfast with the kids and me. They saw that I was okay with that relationship. As time has gone by, it's more and more normal."

It was not perfect. The transitions were still hard, especially for the youngest. Every other week, when Sandy was away and Joe had the kids, the youngest missed her mother.

Yet both parents felt deep satisfaction. Joe said, "They have seen their parents work through the worst of times to be the best that we can be. We both stay involved in their lives. The kids have their struggles like everyone else; and they are creative, expressive, intelligent, and emotionally intelligent. Great people."

Sandy: "They are self-confident. I like my kids so much! I think Joe is a really good father. I like what he contributes to the kids. I am proud that we made a solid choice in our living arrangements, and glad we made it together."

I felt moved hearing how Sandy had one set of struggles, Joe another. Both had to travel a long way from their early anger and grief, and learn how to make it on their own. Both Sandy and Joe noted that they tried harder to grow as individuals after separating than during their marriage. Each made remarkable growth in emotional letting go and self-awareness.

Both were tested to the core as they searched for living arrangements that worked for everyone. Increasing their self-management skills paid off.

Joe and Sandy felt satisfaction and joy about how their children were turning out. This is not to say that their solution will work for everyone, though! I know I could not have lived their choice. But as a rare demonstration of a new possibility, I found it inspiring.

What Do These Stories Tell Us?

All these parents held similar expectations of post-separation parenting when they split, or all were able to reach common expectations. This allowed them to share parenting in widely different arrangements. Zack and Vivian delayed separation so they could support each other in parenting their teenagers. Stefan, influenced by his own father's example, parented his son long distance. In time, he rued the costs of his choice. Gloria's personal growth shifted her approach to co-parenting with Fred, allowing them to find a new equilibrium. Gary and Anna redefined what divorce meant, postponing full, new relationships for themselves to continue their children's experience of family. Joe and Sandy, after three years, found a way to share one dwelling long term.

Joe and Sandy remarked that their growth had made them more effective parents than before. The capacity of growth to strengthen parenting skills will show up again in other stories.

All of these parents functioned at a fairly high level of self-management. Every story had its share of grief and anger to be worked through, but parents sought help to survive this pain and learned from their transitions. These stories emphasize the importance of taking the time to discuss whatever options each parent is willing to consider at any stage in co-parenting. This allows a range of options from which to choose.

The next chapter looks more closely at decision-making in co-parenting.

3 Decision-Making and Ongoing Conflicts

You have to accept whatever comes and the
only important thing is that you meet it with
courage and with the best that you have to give.
— ELEANOR ROOSEVELT

We have already looked at two key aspects of ourselves as parents: our expectations and our self-management skills. A third is our decision-making.

Whether we like it or not, our actions in the first year post-split form the basis of many long-term legal outcomes. These interviews showed that decisions taken in the first year were the most fraught with high emotion, uncertainty, and lack of information about options and their consequences. In other words, our decisions count the most when they are the hardest to make wisely.

And it is hard to know, as we go along, whether we are making good decisions. How are we to be sure? By how we feel? We may not feel good about anything for quite a stretch. Does that mean we're making bad decisions? Not necessarily. By how our ex is responding to our actions, or treating us? Maybe, maybe not.

Perhaps by seeing how the children are doing? But that isn't always easy to discern. If they are babies or toddlers, their actions and moods can be hard to interpret. School-age children won't know what is normal in a family split. They may cover their own unease to avoid upsetting us or sparking family conflict. They won't know when they should reach for help. If their grades fall, or they start acting out, then it's easier to see that they are struggling. More subtle signs are hard to interpret and we may not know for five or ten years how they really are doing.

So it can be very hard to tell if our decisions are wise ones.

What Helps Us Make Good Decisions?

Overall, parents here felt that two actions contributed to good decisions:

1. **Taking their time**
   Parents who took ample time to consider their choices about co-parenting more often believed they had made good decisions.

2. **Seeking information and other perspectives**
   Parents who sought opinions and information from trusted supports felt better about the outcomes of their decisions. Fewer expressed regrets or carried emotional wounds from high-octane encounters.

Co-parenting decisions are made in emotionally charged circumstances. Pauline's and Will's stories below show couples who disagreed on sensitive issues like money, control, and parenting styles. They learned to manage rather than resolve these points, making decisions as conditions changed. Pauline's self-management skills, initially low, led her to make a bad decision. She increased her skills greatly and her parenting changed. Will's situation included his ex-wife's depression, which added extra stresses. Each parent's health and self-management skills affected their interactions.

PAULINE'S STORY:
WHEN YOU DON'T GET RESPECT

control • growth

Pauline's expanded sense of herself and her power changed how she parented her children.

She and Lionel had separated when their children were seven, ten, and eleven years old, three years before she spoke with me. Lionel had been verbally abusive and finally kicked her out of their house. "I was excited to get out. I'd been looking for a way to leave and didn't know how." Not sure what else to do, Pauline agreed when Lionel suggested they do the divorce themselves. She soon regretted her decision. She ended up with only 25 percent time with her children, and had to pay child support, instead of the fifty-fifty time split she wanted.

For Pauline, co-parenting was the only option. "I'm a social worker. I really feel children need both parents in their lives. We owe it to them — we broke up their family. It was nothing to do with them."

Her challenge was co-parenting with someone who didn't respect her. It was hard to accept what seemed so unfair. "My ex didn't respect me or my rules. He told our mutual friend that I'm the babysitter, that I pay *him* money. I wondered if there was any point in trying to communicate with him, and yes, I felt anger."

Her helplessness and frustration came to a head one day when her twelve-year-old was sick at his dad's. He phoned Pauline, asking her to come there and give him some 7Up. She told him, crying, that she couldn't. She called Lionel to ask if she could go over. "He said, 'No, this is how divorce works, Pauline.' I got off the phone and cried for an hour."

Pauline's suffering sparked growth. "I started thinking that we needed to do actual co-parenting. I needed to empower myself. I took co-parenting classes, I read books, and I started therapy. That was a pivotal time. I finally began letting go of trying to control my ex at his house. I realized I couldn't be there for every day of my kids' lives. My mantra now is: I know my ex loves my kids and they'll be okay with him. I have to let go."

She took a different approach in influencing her children, saying they could call her any time, but while they were in Dad's house, it was Dad's rules. "I think they realized then that they have two different houses. Mom can't come and rescue them. Mom isn't going to bash Dad or call him and say, 'What are you doing that for?'"

Pauline's changes built on each other. She took classes and studied so she would know how to co-parent. She learned tools for dealing with Lionel from her therapist and stopped trying to control what happened at his house, which freed up the energy she had spent worrying. She hired a lawyer to renegotiate the parenting agreement.

Feeling more self-confident, she made new parenting choices. Her kids had told her it was confusing to have different bedtimes in the two houses, so she made bedtime the same as in Lionel's house. "They looked at me, sighed with relief, and said thanks. I could have said, 'This is my house and we'll do it my way,' but this is easier for them. I gave up a lot of what I want for my kids so they will be affected as little as possible."

Pauline's Journey

Family and friends made a huge difference for her. She drew closer to her parents, appreciating their financial and emotional support. Her father encouraged her to stop putting herself under stress. Pauline's married friends didn't understand what she was going through, so she found a network of divorced mothers on Facebook and Meetup who knew exactly how she felt. She also appreciated the close friends from childhood who stood by her.

Pauline learned to manage her anger at Lionel differently. "Before, I used to eat, call my parents, and cry to them. I would go home and stuff myself. Then I went back to school, began exercising, and started my business. Now I tell myself, 'I'm going to love my children more than I hate my ex, and walk on the treadmill.' Sometimes I'm on it for an hour and I don't realize it, I just need to walk it off."

Recognizing that her rushed, poorly informed decision had cost her tens of thousands of dollars, she started a business to ensure that others in the same situation would know better. "No one told me what to do, or how to do the divorce. Now I'm using my anger to make sure it doesn't happen to any other women."

Pauline described her growth with pride. "I'm a different parent than when I was married. My ex was controlling and he ruled the house the way he wanted it. I never really figured out my parenting style until I had to. I'm a better parent than I thought I was. This has allowed me to find myself again, to be the person I never thought I could be."

Impacts on the Children

As Pauline's parenting changed, she saw her children relax and grow. "They don't feel nervous anymore at their dad's when he asks them what I am doing. My ex's house is very structured, everything has a time and a place. At my house we get everything done, but we don't have a set time; we hang out and play games a lot. They're becoming well-rounded, learning to have structure but also to take care of themselves when nothing organized is going on."

Hard things remained to worry her. Ongoing legal proceedings had stressed the children; all three had seen a therapist. Two of the children adored Lionel, but twelve-year-old Sam was talking back to his dad, acting out, and getting poor marks. He would call Pauline to come and get him, saying he hated his dad. "Sam has told me repeatedly he never wants to go back to his dad's house. At first I said, 'Oh no, you need to love him' … but I've talked to a therapist and to friends, who said that I need to honour his wishes." The last time he said, "You can't make me stay here," she told him she could right now, but the time was coming when the courts would no longer enforce the rules.

Pauline had recently been given 40 percent time with the children. She felt optimistic that she would reach 50 percent soon and the legal battles would end. She believed the kids were better off in the new arrangement because they got a more well-rounded view of the world, not only their father's. "We do a lot of things we wouldn't have done if I was married. We go different places. It's a huge positive."

Pauline's growth had shifted her perspective. "It's what's good for the kids, not for me. This is how *we're* going to raise our kids together. You can't have it all your way. It's hard to realize you aren't going to be in their lives all the time. You don't have that control; you have to give that up or you'll drive yourself crazy. My new motto is: it doesn't matter. I'm their mother, and they know it."

Pauline deeply regretted her early decision not to get legal advice in divorcing. She was able to recover from it, but it cost her money, time, and heartache. Her strong feelings about the importance of making good decisions prompted her to begin her business helping others make better choices.

Pauline also learned about letting go. In the early co-parenting days, she focused on Lionel's disregard for her and felt great frustration. Then she began to accept Lionel's attitude and make her own choices. Instead of using food to manage her feelings, she learned to exercise and listen to her own voice about what was important. With help from parents, friends, and a therapist, she stopped trying to control Lionel's actions. This letting go lightened her stress load. At the same time, she focused more on what the children needed; they reaped the benefits and she began enjoying her life.

She showed that it's possible to recover from a poor decision through openness, growth, and determination — and that it is not easy, for anyone.

WILL'S STORY:
LEARNING TO MANAGE ONGOING STRESSORS

money • parenting styles • depression

Will, a forty-two-year-old human resources manager, separated from his wife, Ingrid, when their daughters were one and four. He told me his story eight years later. Both parents wanted to prioritize the children's interests but struggled to agree on how to do that. The sensitive topic of money wove in and out of discussions.

Will and Ingrid used trial and error to find a workable schedule post-split. They started with a week-on/week-off arrangement, but it seemed too long, so they tried three days/four days. After two years of experimenting, they agreed on a schedule in which Will had the children from Sunday morning to Thursday and Ingrid had them from Thursday night to Saturday night. They found that a weekly schedule made a good foundation, and they liked having time for themselves, too.

Ingrid had suffered from depression before she had children, and it flared up in the years following the separation. This affected her ability to work and to get the girls to school on time each morning. Depression's unpredictability made co-parenting harder. She would plan to take the girls on an outing, for instance, only to lack the energy to do it when the time came.

Communication and Decision-Making

As the shared parenting evolved, Will learned to step carefully in bringing up changes he thought were needed. "Typically, I took the lead on this; she has always been sensitive of her independence and about my being authoritarian. When we were able to reach an agreement, it was a sign of growth."

Differing styles surfaced when their younger daughter, Bree, was struggling in school because of anxiety, especially during windstorms. "I handled it by talking it through with her, but her mother became fixated on this. She probed the teacher: 'Do you think we should get her assessed?' The teacher said, 'That's always an option.' I bit my tongue." A few days later, Ingrid obtained a referral to a psychologist. Will was angry that she had not consulted him first.

Will struggled to keep open communication, while believing Ingrid was prone to exaggerated responses. He got Ingrid to agree to wait before making the psychologist appointment, but she later changed her mind. "She said sometimes she found it hard to know what to do. The issue seemed to be independence. She was reluctant at first, then said she would cancel the appointment." They had to negotiate periodically when their personalities and parenting styles diverged.

Finances

In *The Road Less Travelled*, M. Scott Peck wrote, "Marriage is never a done deal." Neither is co-parenting, often. For Will and Ingrid, money issues resurfaced, bringing stress and uncertainty.

When they split, Will wasn't sure that Ingrid could provide for their children financially, as she had mainly stayed at home during their marriage. He suggested early that the girls stay with him until she got established. Ingrid strongly rejected that, so they set up a legal co-parenting agreement with Will paying child support. When their divorce agreement was signed, Will felt everything had been settled fair and square.

Eight years later, however, Ingrid, broke and in debt, wanted Will to increase the child support and was hinting at spousal support. Will found it hard to know the right thing to do. He wondered if depression was playing a part. He wanted to be humane, yet he also wanted to keep a predictable limit on his payments to Ingrid. "I can't afford to give her any more money. I am saving for the girls' post-secondary education. It feels precarious, that there may be a battle ensuing. I wonder if she is going to take me to court."

Personal Growth

To survive these challenges, Will sought counselling. His new awareness of his feelings opened the door to his growth. "My default had been to keep a brave face. The first time I broke down, I sat on the floor, crying, and told the girls, 'I'm sorry, I'm feeling sad.' It was scary to just collapse. They came and put their arms around me — it was magical. It was a turning point that drew us closer."

The first year, Will had told a friend how angry and resentful he felt. That Christmas, his friend pointed out an *Incredible Hulk* toy in Toys "R" Us — a set of gloves that, when put on, produced a sound like shattering glass. The friend said, "I think Santa has to bring Daddy these gloves." Will wrapped them up for himself, a symbol of his growth — that he could express his anger and even have fun with it.

Will had a core belief that two parents in a family were better than one, and he missed having a partner to share each day with. Yet he was changing through experience. "We have to be whole and accepting of everything that life brings us before we can be that way with a partner. My weaknesses affect any relationship I am in."

Will's new awareness of how he impacted others — a part of self-management skills — had many benefits. "My self-esteem has increased. I feel free to speak, to share about me with greater comfort. I used to be quite isolated in my own little world. Now I am more relaxed, able to detach from the urgency of things at work."

While money concerns between the parents appear never-ending, Will has drawn comfort that his growth is allowing him to keep managing the challenges and find contentment.

Impacts on the Girls

Right after the separation, Will's daughters cried at night, missing their mother, but then they settled in. Will worried about them. His friends reassured him, saying the girls were well-adjusted.

He saw benefits for his daughters from co-parenting. "The times they see us together are intentional. They don't see as much dysfunction as they would have if we had stayed together. And there's an opportunity for closeness with one parent at a time. Even in my fatigue, lying on the bed thinking I should get up and do the dishes, I can listen to them do their thing. One of them will come in and ask a question or just start talking."

Staying Balanced as Issues Arise

The initial decision to co-parent was easy for Will and Ingrid, but the many decisions that followed tested them. In spite of the stresses, Will felt positive. "Ingrid and I are free now from the crap in the relationship. I believe we're both present and involved in the girls' lives so they don't suffer from lack of one parent or the other. Their needs are being met as best we can."

Will's story highlights how making decisions can be challenging, how depression can add stress, and how growth helped Will. This interview stirred many feelings in me, from admiration and empathy to occasional discomfort with Will's judgments of Ingrid. I appreciated his willingness to name them openly, as we all bring judgments about our exes into co-parenting.

Will's financial health, combined with Ingrid's drive for independence, her depression, and limited earnings caused recurring financial tensions. In spite of the stressors, the parents' self-management skills let them jointly maintain a stable life for their children.

What Do These Stories Tell Us?

Making careful decisions is important. Pauline rued her hasty decision not to use a lawyer when divorcing, and suffered from the resulting meagre contact time with her children. She accessed many supports to broaden her perspective and strengthen herself. She learned how to co-parent long term with a disparaging ex and took action to amend the court ruling. Her children gained a more peaceful family environment.

In Will's case, the decision to co-parent with Ingrid came easily from their shared expectations. However, conflicts surfaced on how best to implement and finance the co-parenting. Will paid attention to how he might be contributing to the conflicts, and sought counselling to understand his feelings so he and Ingrid could make the best possible decisions.

Both Pauline and Will grew in self-management skills, which lessened the conflict with their exes. Both felt satisfied with their children's growth.

The legal system played a minor role in these stories. Pauline wished she had sought her own legal support early on. Will found comfort in knowing he could find solid ground in the law, if necessary. The stories coming up in Chapter 4 contain more intense conflicts and more legal encounters.

4 Extreme Co-Parenting: Intense Conflict and the Court

Perhaps if we saw what was ahead of us, and glimpsed the crimes, follies, and misfortunes that would befall us later on, we would all stay in our mothers' wombs, and then there would be nobody in the world but a great number of very fat, very irritated women.

— LEMONY SNICKET

While co-parenting can bring feelings of joy and contentment to some eventually, many parents in sustained, intense conflict with their ex-spouses often feel unrelenting anger or fear. I found their stories hard to hear. In them, one or both parents acted as if their familiar world was engulfed in flames. Each moment, they did whatever it took to win their way to safety — to a patch of secure, familiar ground.

Feeling powerless to influence the other parent, mothers or fathers often used the legal system to pursue an outcome they believed essential for themselves or their children. However well-meaning, the judges' or officers' actions often seemed misguided and punitive to the parents on the other end of high-conflict disputes. Steep legal fees were only a part of the costs paid.

Brett and Wally both defended themselves in many separate court actions, which drove up their costs. Wally also endured false accusations of molestation, and alienation from his daughter. Francesca and her ex faced off in court repeatedly, which put extended strain on everyone. Carmela faced a co-parent who involved the police to establish his rights, despite the fact that she was intending to share parenting anyway. All four drew on inner and outer resources to survive and find meaning.

BRETT'S STORY:
A LONG DAY'S JOURNEY

years of court • *decision-making*
perspective

"It's been quite a ride." Brett's voice was grey and gravelly.

His story reveals his frustration with the family courts and with how his ex-wife, Shauna, used the law to contest his time with their two daughters. We spoke thirteen years after their marriage had ended. His daughter Tiffany, then eighteen years old, was living with her mother. Rebecca, seventeen, lived with Brett full-time.

Much of Brett's growth came from finding ways to survive painful times, and from thinking about what he wanted to happen. He had learned much more about the legal system than he'd ever wanted to. "We had a difficult six-year marriage; we tried to make it work for the kids' sake, but things came to a head and she got [an] *ex parte** interim custody order." Brett spent two years and $70,000 in legal fees to overcome that custody order, and another five years obtaining a divorce. Shauna went through seventeen lawyers and got six *ex parte* orders, which were all overturned.

Brett assumed that dads would have an uphill challenge in court. "I had to decide whether I would fight this and stay a dad, or forget about it and go live with my brother in Malaysia, have a new life, and connect with the girls in ten years."

He decided that he wanted to be a dad, that his kids needed him. "If the kids grew up with just their mom, it wouldn't be healthy. She's a good person in lots of ways, but she comes by her challenges honestly — had a tough family background."

Then he pondered how he would pursue co-parenting. He decided that whether it cost $500 or $500,000, he would somehow come up

---

* *Ex parte*: one party tells the judge their story, with no involvement of the other party.

with what was needed. "Most times it's reasonable to include finances as a factor, but when we're talking about kids, it's about way more than just money."

First Years: Legal Interventions

Brett's carefully made decision sustained him through encounters with judges, lawyers, and police officers. The first custody order allowed him only phone contact with the girls. The following day, Shauna told a judge that Brett was crazy, suicidal, and abusive. This produced a second order for exclusive use of the matrimonial home, forbidding Brett from having any contact with his daughters.

"Her words were either distorted or a fabrication. The judge was new to the bench and family law. His understanding was based on newspapers, and he didn't consider that someone could be lying. I felt shocked, myself, that someone would lie under oath."

Bailiffs gave Brett five minutes to gather his things before evicting him from the house.

Brett was bounced around by the system like a ball in a pinball machine. He wasn't aware of one *ex parte* order until he received the legal papers saying he was supposed to go back to court two weeks later, in April 2000. He still had no information, no transcripts, and no idea of how to obtain them.

Shauna didn't show up for the April hearing and the judge declined to proceed without her. "I thought that so unfair! The judge had met with her before, when I wasn't present. He adjourned our case till the end of September." Brett got a lawyer who had had one King's Bench order overturned. At the provincial hearing the case was adjourned until December because Shauna had no lawyer. "It was one fiasco after another. She wanted to supervise my visits with the kids. She was in the driver's seat, and I was twisting in the wind."

Brett filed for divorce. One week before the scheduled court appearance, his lawyer changed law firms, moving to the same firm as Shauna's lawyer. This created a conflict of interest, and Brett had to find a new lawyer. Another postponement. Shauna changed lawyers again and agreed to try mediation.

Mediation produced some results. Brett asked for alternating weeks, feeling that the girls would do better with him full-time, but that fifty-fifty would be the best he could get. After two months, Shauna agreed that the kids could be with Brett every other weekend. "I was unhappy, but I went along so I would have some time with them. I thought our arrangement would be for a couple of months." The agreement stayed in force for several years.

Brett and Shauna then had a bilateral parenting assessment done, costing over $10,000. The resulting report recommended that the girls spend the first three weekends of each month with Brett, plus one evening of each week.

The judge accepted the recommendations and the parents began to implement them. Brett felt disappointed, at first, but found unexpected pluses. "Shauna liked having the kids with her during the week. She was not too stressed because she had solo time on the weekends. Having the kids with me on the weekends was fantastic. We had time to do all kinds of things together." Brett finally had some good experiences with his daughters.

A bright spot in all the stress came from Brett's parents. "They were unbelievable. They kept working rather than retire, because I kept having to fork out another ten, twenty, thirty thousand dollars to my lawyer."

Some Resolution and Insight

"When Shauna fired her seventeenth lawyer a few days before the trial, the judge recommended we switch to judicial dispute resolution (JDR),* and we did. The judge read the bilateral parenting report and its update, which stated there was nothing wrong with me as a parent, so I should be at least half-time with the girls. Shauna's emotional challenges were mentioned, but watered down."

During the JDR, the judge asked Brett and Shauna to devise a parenting schedule over lunch break for him to consider. Shauna didn't talk

---

*A JDR is more informal than court, in a boardroom with the judge, parents, and lawyers.

with Brett at lunch. Afterward, when the judge asked for it, Shauna told him, "I can't. I want *you* to decide."

Brett saw that Shauna couldn't come to an agreement with him. "Not only did she not want to come to an agreement, she couldn't." Until then, Brett had believed that Shauna just wanted to push him around. Now he realized that even when she tried, she wasn't capable of taking the steps that could help them both. He softened then slightly, understanding that her actions weren't all deliberately hurtful.

Focus on Parenting: New Challenges

The judge recommended equal time-sharing, and they began a week-on/week-off schedule. Now that Brett could be more fully involved with the girls, he faced ordinary parenting challenges. His older daughter, Tiffany, was not completing projects in her high school work. To provide a consequence for her behaviour, Brett kept her from going on a school trip. "Tiffany got mad at me and said she wanted to live full-time with her mom."

Brett didn't know what to do. Tiffany wanted to live with Brett as long as he made no demands on her. "I wasn't okay with that — video games and telephoning all day. All her life I had struggled to make a difference in her character. It was important for her."

He tried to figure out how he could force her to keep spending some time with him, but realized there was nothing he could do — his daughter would live where she chose. Tiffany moved in with Shauna.

Brett saw little of Tiffany for the next two years, until Brett's sister, visiting, reopened communication between father and daughter. For most of Tiffany's grade twelve year, both girls lived with Brett. Conflict resurfaced the following summer, and Tiffany moved back to her mother's, where she was living when Brett and I spoke.

Only when the parental conflict subsided and the girls began a regular week-on/week-off schedule did Brett have a chance to do what most parents do: try to help their children grow up strong and live with the results. He struggled to balance giving encouragement and setting rules, and learned the limitations of his power as a parent.

Both girls must have been impacted by the years of intense conflict; Tiffany's moving back and forth was a sign of her confusion and anger. Brett's story focused mainly on his own arduous journey, and we didn't talk much about how his daughters were affected.

Making Sense of It All

Brett's growth came through surviving and finding meaning in his suffering. He learned the self-management skills of dealing with his feelings and acceptance. "What I went through was enormously stressful. I had no money — I lived off $180 a month for years, shopping at Value Village. I would get disappointed or frustrated with the courts for not doing the right things. Each time I would just tuck it back up and keep trudging forward. I've learned not to avoid emotions, to let them happen. Emotions are like a hot tub: the bathwater cools off and drains away, and you go about your day. I have accepted that this happened for a reason, and I am supposed to deal with it."

He drew comfort and meaning from the Bible. "Joseph was made a slave, falsely convicted, and thrown into prison. He said, 'This is not fair. What did I do to deserve this?' Later, he became Pharaoh's right-hand man and saved Egypt, and it became clear why all those shitty things had to happen. For me, I decided to help other families from going through what I've been through — that's what makes it worthwhile."

Brett took time to make his initial decision to stay in his daughters' lives. Although he paid great costs both financially and emotionally, he believed he made the right choice. It paid off: eventually, he was able to co-parent his daughters.

By the end of their teen years, both daughters had a genuine connection with their mother and their father; they had lived with them both and knew them well. That base of experience left room for their relationships to develop further. With such sustained conflict between parents, that may be the best outcome we can hope for.

FRANCESCA'S STORY:
DRAMA AND COURTROOMS

repeated legal action

evolving arrangements

Francesca demonstrated courage, anger, and thoughtful decision-making regarding both herself and her children. Numerous legal encounters intensified stresses for everyone.

A high-energy entrepreneur living in Fargo, North Dakota, Francesca reached her limit in her marriage ten years before she spoke with me. Her husband, Wayne, had been travelling a lot, was having an affair, and wasn't around much. "I had been asking him for a divorce for a while and he didn't believe me. I had told my family what was happening and seen a lawyer. I came home one night after talking with a friend and lost it, and threw his suitcase onto the lawn." After chucking clothes and books outside, she realized there was no going back. "I told my mom I was kicking him out, and I called my girlfriends, saying, 'Bring wine!'"

Their daughters were then two and three years old. A Canadian citizen, Francesca stayed in Fargo so the girls would have a relationship with their father. Wayne had the girls every other weekend and one night each week for three years.

Crucible of Conflict

Feelings ran high in the separation. "The first years in Fargo were hell. Wayne closed the bank account and stopped paying the mortgage on our big house. I didn't have a visa so I couldn't work, and didn't have any money. When I told him I needed to buy the kids diapers, he said, 'figure it out.' I sat and cried for days. When I stopped crying, I went into survival mode. A friend's brother thought I was getting badly treated and sent me money."

Wayne and Francesca tried mediation, but it went nowhere. Francesca said, "He wasn't going to let me have anything. I kept saying, 'I'm not caving.'" She wanted child support, but not alimony.

Francesca reopened her business. She saw a child psychologist and a counsellor to ensure she made conscious, informed decisions. After three years, she wanted to move back to Canada, feeling the girls had formed enough of a foundation with their dad.

Their divorce went to court in Fargo. Francesca was afraid. "I had friends but no family there. The courtroom looked like a movie set with a massive bench, and tons of people could come in from the street and watch. There was a heightened sense of drama, which was intimidating."

The final judgment said that Francesca could move north to Winnipeg but required her to drive the girls back to Fargo every other weekend to be with Wayne. Francesca felt relieved, and quickly made the move.

After living a year in Winnipeg, she had a thriving business. The girls, though, were exhausted from driving so much, and the older girl, Jemma, was getting frequent headaches. Francesca refused to keep doing it. "It was easy for him, so complicating for the kids and me." Wayne took her to court and Francesca won. Wayne began driving up to see the girls instead of them travelling to see him.

After another year in Winnipeg, Francesca had begun a relationship with a man, Dave, and the pair wanted to move to Victoria, where most of her family lived. "I sent Wayne a letter of intent. I heard nothing back until I learned, after sixty days, that he had filed papers in Fargo and in Winnipeg."

Another court case began, and lasted three months.

On the Stand

This court case turned into an endurance test for Francesca; she testified on the stand for seven days. "The lawyer ripped apart every one of my friends and said that I was a bad parent. The stories that he made up were mind-boggling. That judge didn't interrupt once. My anger is at the ridiculousness of it, there's no logic to it. Wayne said the girls had headaches because of Dave's dog. Dave had no dog. At one point I passed out on the stand." Then Francesca's lawyer put Wayne on the stand and began to question him. The judge quickly told Wayne to leave. Francesca said with satisfaction, "She knew he was lying."

The judge consulted the girls. Seven-year-old Tasha said, "I love my dad. He buys me stuff so I will tell the judge I want to live with him, but I don't. I want to live with my mom in Victoria."

Waiting for the verdict was agonizing. When the judge gave permission for Francesca to move to Victoria with the girls, Wayne stormed out of the courtroom, saying, "This is bullshit!" At eleven o'clock that night, Francesca was again served with papers saying that Wayne hadn't had enough quality time with the kids and she needed to stay for another six months. They went back to court for two more days, going through the case again.

Her lawyer told her, "Get ready, you're going to win this. Pack, and get tickets so you can get out of here." As soon as they got the positive verdict, they flew to Victoria, where her family waited with balloons to welcome them.

Francesca reflected, "I don't know how I held myself together, but I knew it was in the girls' interest to get them to Victoria, to a stable environment, with the best schools I could afford. There was no way he was going to win. We were not going to live our lives for him any longer."

The recurring tension of courtrooms and expressions of anger reminded me of a television script. I wondered how each family member survived such intensity.

Afterward: Growth and a New Equilibrium

Francesca took eight months to recover from the overwhelming fatigue from the court case. She wondered, *Why did this happen? Why did I marry him?* "I didn't listen to my gut then. Once things slowed down after the divorce, I really took time to understand myself. I knew I would want to be in a relationship again, and I didn't want to be bitter or angry. I wanted a more positive, whole relationship." Eventually, she began a new relationship with Dave, who quickly developed a rapport with her children.

At the same time, two excellent counsellors helped Francesca grow in self-awareness and self-management. "I ... felt great anger at my ex for how he used the legal system against me. I get mad every time I hear women's stories of the ridiculousness of the court system." Francesca decided that she wanted to work with women, channelling her anger into making things better. Life stabilized.

When we met, she said, "It was worth every bit of stress and every penny. Our house is wonderful, the kids' school is wonderful, they are thriving." Francesca and Dave had been living together for five years at that point. As their stepdad, Dave had a close bond with the girls.

For the three years prior to my interview with Francesca, the family had lived a new pattern. Wayne flew to Victoria and spent one week each month with the girls; they also stayed with him for one month every summer. The parents alternated Christmases and other major holidays. For his week each month, Wayne rented a small place near Francesca's house. The girls lived with him, going to school and all their sports games from there. Francesca reported, "They come home exhausted, there are no set bedtimes. But the girls are happy — they want to spend time with their dad; they see lots of him and do lots of sports. They have a good relationship with him, it's like he's a really great uncle."

While Wayne had spent time with his daughters, he wasn't involved in decisions regarding schools or other aspects of their lives. Francesca saw Wayne as not wanting the in-depth parenting role except when the girls were with him, and said, "It's simpler that he doesn't want a lot of involvement. He travelled a lot earlier with his job and wasn't a hands-on parent. He loves his kids, and this is the kind of dad he wants to be. This works for our family."

At ages twelve and thirteen, Francesca said during the interview, the girls were starting to spread their wings socially. Both played soccer and wanted to be at home in Victoria. "Taking them out of their lives is the hardest thing, and this will get harder as they get older. They don't want to go to Fargo in the summer — it's far. We're always talking about how to manage this." The family's pattern will require adjustments.

Intense anger on both sides produced years of volatility and stress for everyone. Repeated recourse to the courts deepened the breach between the parents. At first, Francesca's fury depleted her, until she began to channel her anger into her business. She provided the girls with a stable home, and Wayne's willingness to spend one week each month in Victoria meant the girls spent regular, significant chunks of time with him. His fathering role expanded from earlier years, although it didn't include much decision-making. From a very rocky beginning, the parents found their way to an equilibrium that allowed the girls to know both Wayne and Francesca.

This story doesn't fully meet the criteria for co-parenting, since Wayne doesn't share decision-making, even more recently, as he spent more time with his daughters. It is included because it shows so starkly the consequences of sustained anger. It also highlights the challenges of compromising around physical location, a hard question for many parents.

CARMELA'S STORY:
THE POLICE USED AS AN INSTRUMENT

police • faith • growth

Carmela, thirty-three, spoke with the soft Southern accent of her home state of Virginia. She described her ex, Joseph (they had never married), as an immature manipulator who carried anger from his previous marriage into their current situation with their one-year-old son, Noah. The force of law showed up in their story in two ways: Joseph used the police to ensure his rights, and the legal system helped the parents work together in spite of their intense conflict.

Carmela had become pregnant while dating Joseph but broke up with him before the baby's birth, because she learned he had been cheating. She already had an older, seven-year-old daughter, whose father had left when the child was born. Carmela thought, "If this father, Joseph, wants to be around, well, why not?" and planned to co-parent from the beginning. It wasn't easy, though. Carmela believed that Joseph, angry because she had broken up with him, wanted to attack her through their son.

The day she came home from the hospital after giving birth, Joseph called the police to her house to get a DNA sample and to ensure he would have visitation rights. Sore and weary from birthing, starting to settle her newborn in at home, she found uniformed officers standing at her door. "The police came into my home and looked around. I told them I had just had him and they left. Before I could even suggest that we share custody, Joseph had already filed papers. It was an ugly beginning and a stressful six months in and out of court."

Joseph also called Carmela's employer (she worked with children) and made accusations that she was dangerous. Police traced the phone call and confirmed he had made it.

Despite Joseph's actions, Carmela wanted him to have the involvement with his son that he was seeking. She also wanted to avoid direct contact with Joseph. Their judge appointed a *guardian ad litem* (GAL) for the best interests of the child, and told Joseph not to come to Carmela's house.

Sorting out the child care arrangements exhausted Carmela. "It took a lot of patience and compromise from me — I didn't want any overnights with Noah so little. We tried face-to-face mediation [but] it didn't work because he kept walking out. The GAL took turns talking to each of us to reach an agreement. Joseph doesn't like to compromise. He wanted the baby for three days straight. I said no because I thought he might have to work and wasn't sure what he would do."

The court-ordered compromise evolved; at first Joseph had Noah for a few hours each week, then overnights began, with the GAL monitoring. Joseph had the baby for three overnights each week, Carmela for four. They communicated through email, and Carmela's mother did much of the child care and handled the exchanges, so the mother and father didn't have to come face-to-face. Carmela added, "I'm trying to be civil."

The current arrangement had been in place for six months when Carmela and I spoke. She accepted the situation uneasily. "To me, Joseph doesn't want to spend a lot of time with the baby; he is doing this so he doesn't have to pay so much child support. He often picks Noah up at nine at night, puts him to bed, then drops him right off again the next morning. When Joseph brings Noah back, there is food all over his face. He's not getting proper care over there."

To deal with her anxiety, Carmela turned to her strong religious faith. "I do a lot of prayer. I anoint Noah and pray over him before he goes to his dad's."

Although Carmela worried about how Joseph was caring for their son, she could see how contact with both parents would help in the long term. "When my ex has the baby, I have more time for my older child. I run errands and have a little time to myself. And as Noah gets older, at least he will know his dad. He won't have to wonder about him."

Carmela's Inner Journey

Carmela had released a lot of anger at Joseph over the past year. "I feel sorry for him now. I do pray for him, that someday he gets the peace that he needs. Now when he says something out of line in the book we send back and forth, I just laugh or ignore it. But, I admit, sometimes it still irritates me; it brings back my old self. I don't know why this is bothering me — this is who he is." She was learning the self-management skill of accepting reality.

Carmela now saw the part that she had played. She regretted not finding out more about Joseph before getting pregnant. "If I'd known more about this guy, that he had been convicted of stalking behaviour in his previous marriage, I wouldn't have gotten into this situation. I had to go through counselling to make sure I don't attract someone like him again."

Counselling developed her self-management skills in other areas, too. "I've become a stronger person. I speak up now. At first I got nervous when I had to speak for myself, but now I say what I need to say. No means no. I'm more direct with my family and at work."

Carmela resolved to live differently from now on. "I don't want any more kids until I am married. Having my kids go through two different homes, step-parents — I worry about that. I have a stronger spiritual background, too. I spend more time in prayer and meditation."

Carmela's involvement with Joseph before understanding his character, and Joseph calling the police so early, show low self-management skills. Their actions set up a hard situation. The parents' conflict stayed so intense they needed support from the court system so that they could agree on a way forward. Carmela's mother had a key role as the go-between.

After one year, Carmela had grown. She could defend her interests when needed, while accepting Joseph's right to care for his child. Her religious faith sustained her. Noah was receiving care from both parents, with the GAL supervising. The situation would continue to shift as Noah grew. The arrangement was imperfect, but better than it might have been given its grim start.

WALLY'S STORY: HELPLESS IN THE FACE OF FALSE ALLEGATIONS

> *many depositions • accusations of molestation alienation*

Wally and I met in a coffee shop for his interview. A grey-haired, rumpled man, tension and grief from the past twelve years never left his voice. Though he was able to achieve shared parenting for some years, his ex had never stopped denigrating him to their daughter, and Wally felt he had lost his relationship with his child.

Wally's wife, Sonia, ended their marriage after only three years, when their daughter, Meg, was two. "We had three years of being apart in a fairly civil relationship. We were trying to put things together but not willing to take counselling; our hearts weren't in it. I saw Meg and her mother regularly, several times a week. I would take them both out for dinner sometimes. It seemed quite normal, except I wasn't living at the house."

Then Wally got a letter from a lawyer and everything changed. "Events took a huge slide downhill. Once lawyers were involved and accusations started flying, the relationship became bitter. When we got to court, we had a lot of acrimony and huge lawyers' fees."

They spent twenty-two days in trial, at thousands of dollars a day. It was expensive for Wally but not for Sonia, because she was on social assistance and used legal aid. Wally believed that if their situations had been more equal, there would have been less litigation. "She was free to explore her imagination." He spent more than $150,000 on legal fees, defending against forty-three depositions; he had to answer each one separately. Sonia used nine different legal aid lawyers, dropping one and then obtaining another.

Her most painful accusation was that he had sexually abused their daughter. Wally said, "Of course this was false. But once she said that, there were thirteen months when I had no contact at all with Meg."

Wally, a church chaplain, received support from a peer group of chaplains and ministers. Friends came with him to the many court hearings where he defended himself against allegations of abuse. He also joined a group of fathers struggling with custody issues, where he gained moral support, a place to vent, and knowledge he wasn't alone.

After all the legal hoops and court days were finished, the judge offered Wally full custody of his daughter. Wally felt hugely relieved. He believed, though, that children need both parents and that Sonia was a good caregiver, so he opted for fifty-fifty custody, alternating weeks. He lived to regret it.

"My ex continued to look for ways to undermine my parenting, and I felt under scrutiny for every action. I got worn down, so I was less firm in setting limits with Meg than I would otherwise have been."

He also believed that Sonia never accepted the shared arrangement, and that she continued to disparage him to Meg, thus putting huge pressure on their daughter.*

The arrangement of alternating weeks lasted for six years. Wally enjoyed it. "It gave me time to be a doting father, preparing nice meals every night and providing Meg with a room with a TV and internet. It

---

*It is widely accepted that putting a child in the position of having to choose sides between their parents is destructive to him or her. If one parent disparages the other parent enough to turn the child against the other parent, it is called *parental alienation*.

also gave me private time when I could be a bachelor." He was satisfied that Meg had lots of contact with both parents. "I know her mother takes good care of her, and loves her."

Sadly, at fourteen, Meg chose to live with her mother full-time. Wally didn't use the word *alienation*, but he believed that Sonia had succeeded in turning Meg against him. When Wally and I met, he had regular contact with Meg, but not a lot. He seemed to be withdrawn and he carried a pervading sense of loss. He held little hope for a future bond with his daughter.

Lessons Learned

Wally reflected, "If I had to do it again, I would not have agreed to fifty-fifty. I'd have taken the chance to have full custody myself so my ex couldn't keep trying to get revenge on me."

Ten years later, Wally still feels baffled at his ex-wife's allegations of abuse. He knows Sonia desperately wanted custody of their daughter, but he doesn't understand how she could bring such serious false accusations against him. "Did she get it, that I could have gone to prison as a sex offender?" In the men's group he facilitated for eighteen months, Wally asked how many had had allegations of sexual abuse made against them. "Of the total of eleven men, eight raised their hands. There was such a sense of shame and frustration."

He still sees Sonia as basically a good person who had been negatively influenced by a group she joined. Much of his anger is directed at the legal system. "It is so adversarial that it brought conflict to a fine point."

Wally learned some positive things. He has become more patient. "I have more empathy and compassion, especially for addictions. I have a greater sense of my humanness, and that of others."

Growth can be joyful to witness, but not always. In this interview, Wally's changes had arisen from such stark pain that I wanted to look away. Wally struggled to keep his answers focused on his parenting of Meg, but scars from the false allegations and court processes still haunted him, and many of his responses turned back to the legal battering he had endured.

Wally created meaning in his experience through working with other men facing similar situations. "If something good were to come out of this, it would be for fathers to become more patient, and for the courts to learn to use mediation more."

What Do These Stories Tell Us?

You, like me, may have felt sad and angry reading these mothers' and fathers' stories. They show it's not a simple matter of "good guys" versus "bad guys" — more like each person wading into the turmoil of separation and divorce, equipped with whatever levels of self-management and awareness they possess.

Some parents took dramatic steps that threatened or humiliated the other parent. Francesca's throwing her husband's belongings outside and Joseph's sending the police to Carmela's house the day she came home from the hospital likely intensified the cycles of protective, hostile behaviours. Brett and Wally both experienced multiple court processes and accusations, against which they defended themselves at a cost of hundreds of thousands of dollars.

We also heard anger and deep helplessness about court systems. When negotiation between parents failed, one or both turned to the courts as a necessary alternative. Yet parents found the courts damaging in two ways. The court system itself, with its adversarial foundation, often made things worse. It intensified antagonism instead of promoting reasoned action. The system was also open to manipulation and abuse through false accusations and repeated procedural delays.

The stories didn't include many details of how the children were impacted, as parents' energies were often drawn to handling the conflicts. It's hard to imagine that there would be no lasting effects on them. When conflict burns intensely over many years, it's hard to know what success looks like. These parents gathered their resources and supports around them to survive the stress and do their best for their children. Brett and Carmela found comfort in their faith. Over time, Francesca and Carmela sought help to improve their self-management skills and understanding. Brett, Francesca, and Wally found meaning in their struggles by using their experiences to help other families avoid such distress.

Each of these parents found a way to provide love and relative stability for their children, regardless of the financial and emotional impacts on themselves. They grew in patience, self-understanding, and confidence. They reached for constructive responses to painful events, and kept going.

The next chapter examines addictions, which can also bring legal, financial, and emotional factors into play.

5 Co-Parenting with Addictions

Wherever you go, there you are.
— JON KABAT-ZINN

An addiction is like an iceberg: much of its impact lurks below the surface of daily life. It can cast a deep chill on the spousal relationship by adding unpredictability and lowering self-management, which erodes intimacy. Financial health often declines. Addiction to alcohol, drugs, or gambling doesn't necessarily create extreme events, but as millions of attendees of Al-Anon and Nar-Anon meetings demonstrate, it takes a toll on partners and families. Co-parents grapple with how to support a child's relationship with the other parent while minimizing the costs or risks to children living with an addict.

The words *addict* and *alcoholic* are used with varied meanings. To one person, they describe a consistent overuse of a substance or an indulgence in a habit, one that strains family and relationships yet still lets the person hold a job and cope on a surface level. To another person, they refer to someone who has hit bottom and can seldom or never function normally. Most of us have our own definitions of these terms, which may not be the same as those telling these stories.

The three stories that follow highlight different impacts of addictions. Janice grappled with the risk of her daughter riding in the car with her father when he might be drunk. She felt caught between fear, court-ordered co-parenting, and belief that her daughter needed to know both her parents. Patrick lived many uneasy years, aware of volatility and lack of focused parenting from his ex-wife. Only when he learned to take a stand could he provide a clear set of expectations for his sons. Genevieve's story shows how focusing on her own role expanded her self-confidence and supported a stronger relationship with her ex, in spite of big financial stressors.

JANICE'S STORY:
MAKING THE BEST OF A HARD SITUATION

drinking • the courts • growth

Janice came to the door of her rental unit to greet me. In the West Coast mid-winter, the wet grass of her tiny backyard was littered with toys. We stepped into a clean, cramped living room overflowing with puzzles and children's books.

Janice, her brown hair framing her alert face, looked younger than her forty-two years. Her chin lifted with pride as she described her degree studies in occupational therapy, her road to a meaningful career. When she started talking about her seven-year-old daughter, Kelly, her face tensed.

Janice had left her second marriage four years before. Both of her husbands had been abusive. She was co-parenting with Kelly's father, Paul, her second husband. He had care of Kelly Wednesdays and Thursdays of most weeks, plus some Sundays. She shared parenting with mixed feelings.

"We were pushed into the court system due to concerns about previous violence, and Paul's drinking and driving. We had had fights with police involvement. When I left, I got a full restraining order for a year. Otherwise, he would have come to wherever I was and taken Kelly away. The order lasted long enough for things to calm down."

Janice didn't believe that Paul was always sober when he drove with Kelly in the car, yet the courts had ordered the parents to share time. She found the court's decisions unreasonable because her concerns about

Paul's alcoholism had been dismissed. "The judge was a father's-rights type who looked at me as if I was exaggerating. I had brought witnesses. I know he drinks and drives — I can't really be the watchdog. I almost have to trust that it's all going to be okay for her." She felt helpless to protect Kelly and still respect the court's ruling.

Janice hugged her arms tightly around herself. "I'm mad at him a lot because he doesn't do his job with Kelly. There's usually chaos at his place. He likes to set up fun activities, but doesn't do daily care, like brushing teeth or bathing. She often comes back in the same clothes she left in and hasn't washed. Kelly knows her father doesn't have the same presence and attention as I do — he's not there. She comes home and spills the beans. I try to stay neutral and support him, though some choices he makes are ridiculous. He showed up drunk at Kelly's school one day to pick her up. Kelly doesn't know that; another parent stepped in and brought her home."

Janice understood, too, that some of Kelly's days with her dad were fun — it wasn't all bad. "He offers her a different way of living. And no matter how strained their relationship, she needs to know who her parents are."

Finances were tough. When she left her second marriage, Janice had to go on social assistance for six months until she found a minimum-wage job. Paul had continued to run his business, so he was financially stable. He contributed some support, and usually covered a cost for Kelly if Janice asked him to. After three more years her training would finish, and Janice expected to earn a good living. Until then, though, money was sparse.

Managing Impacts on Kelly

Janice tried to speak neutrally about Kelly's dad to her, knowing that to do otherwise would put pressure on Kelly. She seldom spoke about Paul's drinking, as she didn't want to sound like she was putting Paul down. Sometimes Kelly called from her dad's place, saying, "Mommy, I miss you," and Janice would stay on the phone, counselling her. Janice tried to strengthen Kelly by teaching her to ask directly for what she needed. "She seems to be learning."

As well, Janice's return to school helped Kelly to see her mother in a powerful way. "Watching Mom be passionate and work hard — that's empowering for kids. Not seeing me trampled down."

She sensed a contrast between how she and Paul dealt with Kelly. "My daughter's experiences with her dad make us closer because she sees how different I am with her. Every day she says how much she loves me. I know I'm her rock." Janice's brown eyes filled with tears.

Janice's Growth

Having married two abusive husbands, Janice was learning to make better choices. "I had no access to money while I was married to Paul. I was losing all sense of who I was. I didn't feel connected to my life, I felt vacant." Six months after leaving Paul, she was seeing a great guy. "I am happy I had the opportunity to move on. My life is my own."

She slowly learned skills like how to speak up about her needs. She had belonged to a peer counselling group for sixteen years where she took her anger and upset feelings. "It's been my lifeline. I sing, and write songs, that's a healing thing … and do lots of journaling." She feels more confident. "I used to take everything personally. I've learned I'm capable of doing anything I put my attention on. I feel smart now."

Janice's story began with poor financial health and an ex-husband drinking heavily, with some instances of violence. Her recent decisions demonstrated how she's grown. She chose a non-abusive partner and was earning credentials for a good career. She was applying her improved self-management skills to deal with her anger and distress. She was teaching skills to her daughter, like asking for what she needed. Yet her worry remained about co-parenting with Paul. She didn't want to flout the law by going against the court order, but she didn't always trust Paul to keep Kelly safe. In far-from-ideal circumstances, she made the best choices she could.

Janice was following a path I could understand, if not feel comfortable with: when we are not sure what else to do, we keep doing the same things. In the chapter on decision-making, we saw that seeking input from others helps us make good decisions. Janice had turned mainly inward for sustenance through her journaling and singing, except for her peer support group. While Janice grew significantly, she may have developed even more and seen more options if she had sought outside resources specific to alcoholism.

PATRICK'S STORY: FINDING HIS BEST PATH

volatility • new skills • structure

Computer programmer Patrick and his wife, Ruby, had been married six years and had five-year-old twins when their marriage ended. Now in his sixties, Patrick tapped into his memories from thirty years earlier for our interview. His story showed how Ruby's volatility and Patrick's easy-going nature influenced their co-parenting, and how his growth made a difference for the boys.

The marriage hadn't been going well, so Patrick breathed easier when the couple decided to separate. They agreed to share time week-on/week-off. Patrick said quietly, "We made a commitment to live close to each other. I would have preferred sole custody of the boys, but if I'd tried for more, it would only have been a fight. I was relieved and satisfied to reach an agreement that was equitable and would work for Seth and Seamus — especially us living close together."

When they separated, Patrick stayed in the family home and Ruby moved into a house down the street with a man Patrick knew. Patrick talked with the boys about the separation, emphasizing that it wasn't their fault.

The new arrangement sort of worked, but Patrick soon became concerned about the volatility of Ruby's romantic relationship. "She was hitting the bottle pretty hard for a while. The pair often fought. If it became uncomfortable, Seth or Seamus could call and I would get them out, if I happened to be there. I talked with the boys quite a bit about their mom's situation, reassuring them they were safe, that they could come over at any time, that everything would be okay. They were never physically unsafe."

The parents remained friends. "Ruby and her new partner didn't seem to mind my involvement. I was glad it wasn't me in the fights."

Patrick found his parenting role a challenge as it was hard to maintain consistency. He thought that if he didn't provide it, it wouldn't be there. "I liked the week-on/week-off because, on my week off, I didn't have to rush to be home. But it made things more difficult for the week on. I'd have fallen behind on making sure that school work was done and catching up on what had happened. My impression, and it may not be completely fair, was that Ruby wasn't doing much monitoring. Ruby wasn't the most consistent parent. She adored the boys, but that wasn't always enough. I worried."

A self-described easygoing guy, Patrick sometimes felt angry at Ruby for her lack of consistency with Seamus and Seth. He didn't know what to do about it. "I didn't handle it at all. I could show displeasure with her, but I couldn't get angry. She was so volatile that if I expressed anger openly, it would start a fight that wouldn't go anywhere. You kind of get trapped. You have feelings, but you can't express them."

While Patrick often felt vague unease about the boys, Christmas was a bright spot. "We would all have Christmas together for a while, and that worked really well."

The equilibrium lasted for ten years and then faltered. Ruby and one of the boys, Seth, shared a temper and started to clash when Seth was fourteen. "He was a handful. Ruby and her boyfriend took road trips to neighbouring towns with the boys. She would have a fight with Seth, or he would pick one with her, and she'd kick him out of the car. Seth called me from a pay phone a few times and I had to go get him. Once, I found him at a service station with only a jean jacket on."

Patrick called Ruby. "Seth called me again today, from the gas station at Cardston where you'd left him. It's no place for him. What happened?"

Ruby replied, "Seth got so lippy I just lost it. He doesn't listen! He was okay, wasn't he?"

"Well, yes, he didn't come to harm. But he could have, Ruby. You can't keep doing this."

"If only he didn't push my damn buttons! Yeah — it won't happen again."

But it did. Periodic conflicts between Ruby and Seth lasted for over a year, with Patrick's anxiety mounting. Then Ruby left Canada for a job in Thailand. The twins moved in full-time with their father, who by now had remarried.

The remarriage added stress for the boys, though both got along well with Patrick's wife and baby. Each twin responded differently to the changes. Seth seemed insecure and private, spending a lot of time in his room playing computer games. Seamus played football and soccer; this seemed to help him find a place in his school. Patrick was less concerned about Seamus than about his brother.

He was right to worry. Seth stopped going to school, leaving the house each morning and spending time with friends. When Patrick discovered this, he told Seth to get back to school or get a job or leave. Seth moved out and lived with a friend. He would stay with Patrick after that for visits, but never lived long term in Patrick's house again.

Ruby's situation changed, too. Patrick learned that during her eighteen months in Thailand, she had started using hard drugs. When she returned to Canada, she rented a house near Patrick's, but her relationship with her sons never recovered. "The time abroad doing drugs hadn't helped her psyche — she had gotten a little weird. The boys never seemed to regain their trust in her." Two years later, Ruby remarried and moved to a town five hundred kilometres away.

Seth finished his education, including college, while living with a friend's family. Seamus finished high school and headed to university in the U.S. At interview time, both grown sons were living within a half-hour of their father's house. Each had a good relationship with him. Seth had twin daughters, with whom Patrick was close.

Patrick's Growth as a Parent

Patrick, not naturally one to take firm stands, had qualms for years about the inconsistent expectations on the boys and the conflict between Ruby and Seth. His concern deepened, but he felt uncertain about what to do. Finally, when the boys were fourteen, he started seeing a therapist who helped parents deal with difficult teens.

Patrick then realized that he needed to fill the void of structured expectations for his sons, and learned to take a stand. "The best thing I did in all this was the therapy and getting clarity for myself in dealing with Seth's temper. If I hadn't done that, I don't know what would have happened. I needed to have confidence in what I was doing. I had to be an authority in their lives — to be clear and draw the line somewhere, eventually. That's not in my nature, so that was a change. Seth in particular had some hard lessons to learn. I think it benefited the boys. They're both great guys now."

If Patrick could have spoken to his earlier self, he would have said, "You have to say what's expected and see that that happens. Take a leadership position sooner. I didn't realize that for children to feel secure they need a fortress to butt up against. If I'd been less flexible, they'd have felt more secure."

This was a hard situation. Ruby's use of alcohol and later drugs, combined with her short temper, made the family system unstable. Patrick's laid-back style and Seth's temper also played a part. Patrick learned to step in and set clear expectations for his sons, fostering their development and strengthening their bond with him. Sadly, Ruby's sustained volatility and drug use seemed to erode the connection and trust between her and the boys.

GENEVIEVE'S STORY: FINDING PEACE

money • control • family patterns

It wasn't lack of money that drove fifty-year-old Genevieve to leave her marriage, but the resulting fights with her husband, Louis, that were scaring their two-year-old son, Paul. "We were sitting in the living room, arguing, and Paul stood between us and put his little hands in the air crying, 'Stop!' That was it. I knew this was the wrong way for him to grow up."

Finances stood out neon-bright in Genevieve's story. After twenty-one years together, the couple's divorce had been underway for four years and was not yet complete at our interview. Genevieve sighed. "It's been a long process. I knew I wouldn't get one red cent from Louis unless I went to a lawyer and actually did proceedings. It's cost me almost $20,000 and it's the best money I've ever spent. It's hard in the short term, but the support money will make a big difference for our son by the time he's eighteen."

At first, Genevieve simply wanted get away from Louis. "I didn't think about co-parenting. He wouldn't move out of the house, so I went back to live with my mom. I felt angry — I had married my dad! Louis was an alcoholic, a gambler, a drug user. He went through money over and over in our marriage. I never saw where things were going. I thought he'd get out of his addictions, that I wouldn't divorce like my parents had."

Accepting that she had repeated her parents' pattern hit Genevieve hard; she became depressed and had a breakdown, going into the hospital for several days. Genevieve faced severe financial challenges as she recovered. "I left in June. I had just finished paying off his last debt of $40,000, which had been with loan sharks and biker gangs. Because he had no credit, I had the loan in my name; his paycheque was coming to me and I paid him an allowance. Louis wouldn't agree to sell the house unless I assumed the $58,000 loan on the house in my name. I said yes."

A month after separating, the parents met to discuss the future. Each had a lawyer and a counsellor to support the collaborative divorcing. Genevieve didn't seek co-parenting, assuming that Louis would have Paul every second weekend. "Louis wanted fifty-fifty sharing because then I would be paying him; I make more money than he does." Early divorce discussions were heated. "The money was a sore spot for me over the twenty years. I saw red a lot!" One last challenge nearly sank the agreement. Louis's lawyer said that Genevieve's account was out by $14,000, which Louis had borrowed from family and friends. "I said he wasn't getting any more from me and walked out of the room. I had a $58,000 debt and they were telling me I had to pay more! I felt sick."

The lawyer followed up a few days later. When Genevieve threatened to bring in Louis's DUIs* and drugs and take him to court, Louis withdrew the $14,000 from discussions and they settled. Louis's work shifts wouldn't accommodate having Paul equal time, so he had Paul every second weekend and two to four afternoons or evenings per week.

Because Louis had Paul less than half of the time, he paid some child support. "Even now, he doesn't think he should owe me anything; he thinks I'm taking trips on his money. Once when he started on about this, I snapped, 'You give me less than $500 a month and Paul's daycare is $550. So shut up.' I wasn't going to take his son away from him, I just wanted some support."

Money, Control, and Trade-Offs

Genevieve reflected on how finances dominated her thinking. "I'm a money person, because with my parents being alcoholics, that's all the control I had." She worried, now, about Paul's future. "We have alcoholism from both sides of the family. My ex is still drinking. I'm getting Paul into sports so when he is older that will hopefully be a focus for him. I want to bring him into the church, too, so he will have something else to do on Sundays besides hang out at his dad's and drink."

Genevieve still focused on money but had learned to step back, somewhat. "I finally had to look inward and say to myself that it's only money. The loan is now down to $26,000. I know that once it's paid, my anchor to him will be gone and our son will be the only thing still between us. We live cheque to cheque because I am paying down that loan. He got off scot-free."

Once she had vented her frustrations and worries, Genevieve described the upsides of co-parenting. "I don't think I was cut out for single parenting. One night Paul threw up on the sheets, then on the next set of sheets, then on the rug, and then in the sink. I didn't know they could throw up that much!"

She needed downtime. "By the end of the week I am ready to tear my hair out. It gets so bad sometimes I give myself my own time out! You are

---

*Driving Under the Influence (drunk driving) charges.

so at your wit's end, your child is saying, 'I hate you.' Time alone gives me the chance I need to regroup. Louis taking Paul those times gives me sanity so when I am with Paul I have a smile on my face. I take more pleasure in him."

Their co-parenting had evolved in several ways. "Louis used to play fight with Paul, until Paul hit one of the daycare workers. Then there was trouble! At that point Louis listened to me about how we need to teach Paul to use his words. When Louis got frustrated with Paul, he used to call me and bring him back. After a few times, I told Louis to keep him and figure it out."

Genevieve could now see Louis more clearly. "Louis is a good dad, kind of the Disney dad. He will play with Paul on the ground, make a whole castle; he plays with him differently than I do. I can't play dinosaurs with Paul. Louis is just not going to be a good role model. Paul will see him drinking and going to parties. Louis is over forty now and hasn't grown up."

> Addictions are common in Western society; they can be isolating and devastating. If these stories seemed familiar to you, or you struggle with the same issues, remember that Al-Anon, Nar-Anon, Alcoholics Anonymous, and other sources of support can help. Al-Anon and Nar-Anon support people impacted by the alcohol use or drug habits of others. You can find them at www.al-anon.org, www.nar-anon.org, and www.aa.org.

Genevieve's Personal Growth

Individual and group counselling, plus support from her pastor, increased Genevieve's self-management skills. "I had a lot of counselling. I found a personal change program that taught me you can only change yourself. I had to learn this before I could move ahead."

Her communication skills improved. "I used to blow up. That didn't help. I have been learning to use *I* statements. Every now and then I think it's all in how you talk to people."

She felt new confidence in her strength. "I am determined; I put my mind to a goal and follow it through. When I got into the apartment, we had nothing but a couch and a TV on the floor. Now we've got all new furniture, a console, and a new TV. Living through this has showed me I am strong, I am a mother, I can do it."

Her new confidence changed how she parented Paul. "Before, I had a negative attitude, thinking I can't do this, I can't do that. Anytime there was a problem with Paul, I thought I was failing. I put it all on me, like a huge weight on the back of my head. Now I say I did the best I could. If I make a mistake, I talk to Paul about it and say, 'Mommy made a mistake.'"

A Mixed Bag of Outcomes

"Paul has both his dad and me. At pizza night at the school, all three of us sat on the gym floor, watching the movie. Every once in a while, Paul will ask why we don't live with Daddy. I say, 'This way you get two happy homes to go to, instead of one unhappy home.'"

Overall, Genevieve felt satisfied with where she was. "I can dream again; I have a spirit. I am happier." Yet she knew that the example of alcohol and drug use set by Louis could lead Paul in that direction later. And despite all her growth, she believed that she and Louis would never see eye to eye on finances. "We can't talk about money, we just can't. When that loan is paid off, we will move into a house. We will have a life."

What Do These Stories Tell Us?

The heavy use of alcohol or drugs resulted in money problems, volatility, and some violence. Janice had concerns about Kelly's safety when driving with her father, yet felt bound by court decisions and her belief that Kelly needed to know both of her parents. She was modelling self-reliance for Kelly and teaching her skills, yet she was trapped by conflicting constraints.

It was an accomplishment for someone as naturally laid-back as Patrick to learn to set limits with a temperamental teen. Improving his self-management skills led Patrick to intervene confidently with his sons and provide consistent limits, which promoted their growth.

Genevieve faced daunting debts and low self-confidence when she left her marriage. With help, she shaped a new life, paid down her debts, and reduced the conflict her son experienced. Fears remained about her ex as a role model, but she built as strong a life for her son as she could.

I felt disturbed by Janice's and Patrick's decisions to keep co-parenting when safety concerns arose for their children. And I understood that they were struggling to find the best course of action amid scarce options. The addiction of one parent led to unpredictability for everyone. Patrick and Genevieve enlarged their options by learning new self-management skills from external sources. I admired the courage of all three parents in focusing on what they could control and being effective in those areas. Each became a stronger parent through their growth.

6 Co-Parenting with Mental Health Conditions

*Mental illness leaves a huge legacy, not just for
the person suffering it but for those around them.*
— LYSETTE ANTHONY

Health problems are wild cards in the game of life. While we can do things to strengthen our minds and bodies, illness and long-term conditions can still occur, sweeping us onto paths we never imagined. When troubles arise, our ability to care for ourselves and our children depends on both our own health and the health of the other parent.

Mental health issues test us in two ways. First, our minds are critically important because they let us understand our complex world and choose appropriate behaviours. Second, mental conditions are not visible; they may never be recognized by ourselves or by those around us. Lack of understanding has led to a stigma about mental illness that is only slowly diminishing.

This chapter has only one story, although a common condition, depression, shows up in other chapters, such as with Will in Chapter 3. Ed's story here shows a father who co-parented with a woman struggling with volatile moods, depression, and the after-effects of a concussion. He wanted to provide a healthy environment for their daughter in a way that respected his ex's needs (as he understood them) and his own.

ED'S STORY:
PHYSICAL AND MENTAL STRESSORS

volatility • entrepreneurship
depression • concussion

Ed at forty-seven was an easygoing craftsman with an introspective air. We talked two years after his separation from Daphne. He was immersed in learning how to manage their volatile relationship in a way that minimized impacts on their daughter, Charlene, who was then eight.

Early in their marriage, Ed had started a business in Mission, British Columbia. His struggles as a new entrepreneur strained his relationship with Daphne. "I wasn't good at removing the craftsman hat and putting on the businessman hat when I needed to, so there was a lot of stress. I was always working, even at home. Daphne would say, 'I've called you three times for dinner.' It wasn't a pretty scene."

Other factors contributed to the tension. Throughout their marriage, Daphne suffered from long-term, moderate depression. Ed experienced her as explosive and unpredictable. As well, Daphne experienced a severe concussion in an accident two years before they separated. Lingering after-effects prevented her from working — she needed to nap often in order to manage her intense headaches.

Friction between them brought Ed and Daphne close to separating, and Ed had an affair. "Our big disruptions came from me banging another woman — not whether I put enough cheese on her macaroni. I was always trying to manage Daphne's temper; I thought she was a 'rageaholic' and that I could influence this. I've learned that sometimes this backfired. I didn't want to pick a fight, and she was all about picking fights."

Events one night tipped the scales for Ed when Daphne attacked him as he was leaving the house. "Charlene witnessed it and cried out, 'Mommy, stop, stop! I'm on Daddy's side!' It was such a heavy night. I decided I was done with the relationship. I took Charlene to my mom's that evening after the police came and the dust settled. When I saw the act of violence, I realized I couldn't contain any longer whatever had gotten out. I moved out for my safety and for the effect on Charlene."

Ed felt confident that Daphne's temper came out only at him, so he agreed that Daphne would be the primary parent. Both parents stayed closely connected to Charlene. "I wondered how Charlene would fare in a separation, but it's worked well. Daphne's a dedicated and enthusiastic mom. Even with her disdain for me, Daphne knew I was good for Charlene and wanted me to be her father. There was some overriding principle she couldn't ignore."

Initially, Ed was afraid of being denied access to Charlene because of his infidelity. "It was I who sinned. I was afraid Daphne might move to the interior of British Columbia, where she had family. The thought of having to drive to Westbank from Mission terrified me — it's a grind. I'd seen Daphne's brother doing this kind of commute."

Instead, Daphne got a basement suite near Ed in Mission, stabilizing the living arrangements. "I felt like I'd won the lottery when I heard her new address, a half-hour drive away. Charlene likes my new space, but her home and her stuff are with her mother." Ed had Charlene for three-day weekends every other weekend, plus other visits.

In the two years post-split, Ed didn't yet feel they had reached a steady state. Sudden blazes of conflict kept requiring negotiation. "I'm still in full-armour mode in Daphne's presence. I would like to live closer to her. I've even considered moving into their building so Charlene could have almost the real thing. But I've never raised it because there hasn't been calm water. Every day feels like a win."

Finances felt tricky, too. They had no separation agreement, though they had been working on one for two years. Daphne removed all the money from their joint account after they sold their house, leaving Ed feeling like the rug had been pulled out from under him. Within Ed's anger lurked chagrin that he had partly allowed it to happen. "I freaked out, saying, 'What are you doing? We haven't talked about this!' Well, she took half. That showed she was aware of the principles. I left my half in the joint account and she eventually took it, too. What an idiot. I was pretty pissed, but I know this will work out."

Co-Parenting Patterns

The unpredictability between Ed and Daphne persisted. At every hand-over from mother to father, Ed feared being blindsided by an unfore-seen demand or expectation. "The weather systems would blow in out of nowhere. I'm at the door to get Charlene. The bags are in my hand. Daphne says, 'You have the thermometer?' and just a certain roll of my eye is all that's required for the deadbolt to be turned and Daphne to say, 'There's no fucking way you're taking my daughter out that door.' Volatile! We've had a few of those."

Ed found their parenting styles divergent. "I have to go along and smile and suck up the differ-ences in parenting. We just got through the birth-day party. It was almost like a military flyby in its grandeur, so over the top. For Charlene's sixteenth birthday, I can see Daphne saying, 'Maybe we can put her in orbit? There must be a space station that takes bookings!'"

Depending on your location, some mental health resources may be offered free, and others will have a price tag. Community resource centres often provide counselling at no or low cost. Here are some sites: www.dbsalliance.org, www.obad.ca, www.helpguide.org, and www.psychcentral.com.

Daphne's depression and concussion symp-toms didn't cause any specific problems that Ed could identify. Their effects were more general and pervasive. "The extra stressors were like two more blocks in the backpack of weight we have carried."

In spite of the difficulties, Ed liked shared parenting. "Our routine works pretty well. We alternate Christmas and Thanksgiving. In summer, the three-day weekends feel much bigger. Lots of beach time. Charlene has learned to ride a bike, so we go around the park."

Ed's new partner, Shelley, had a clearly defined role with Charlene. "Charlene has quite a crush on Shelley. It's so great. I think, *Somebody pinch me*. I have no expectation of Shelley taking on a mothering role. Shelley's kids are grown and she has no wish to go through that again. Boundaries are clear both for Charlene and Shelley."

Ed sounded comfortable with the time and quality of the relation-ship he had with Charlene. He felt he was so present with Charlene when they were together that he didn't need as much time with her as

Daphne had. "I get the better-looking part of time with her — her mom gets a bit stuck with the drudgery, like laundry and discipline. Charlene and I have good connection time. She packs her bag and we have great adventures."

He conceded that he was more lax with Charlene than Daphne was. "The cliché that daughter has Dad wrapped around her finger? There may be some truth in that. Anything bohemian is more my style. We'll lounge around eating grapes and a lot of popcorn. We get along famously. Our conversations may seem too grown up, but she isn't showing signs of that."

Impacts on Charlene

While content with his time and relationship with Charlene, Ed believed she was overweight and thought her diet should be different. "I abdicate most parenting decisions to Daphne; she's a fantastic mom and her heart's in the right place. But there are some things I would like to have influence on. I believe I will be able to model those things and, in time, impact Charlene."

He saw costs to his daughter of ongoing clashes between her parents. "Charlene got the message real quick that she can influence our interactions. If I set a boundary with Daphne, Charlene steps right in to smooth things over. She'll put aside her desires and say, 'No, it's okay, I don't want that anymore.' Neither Daphne nor I want her to do that, at eight years old. Yet we still create the environment for that to happen."

Generally, Ed felt that Charlene was doing well. "She is facing the world with two solid anchors in her life. It's not the same as it used to be, and she'll remind us once in a while that she misses the experience of a nuclear family. But overall, our arrangement meets her needs. She's a delightful, connected child."

Ed's role as father held contradictions. He was comfortable being the more relaxed, fun dad, abdicating many parenting decisions to Daphne, yet he also wished for more influence on aspects of Charlene's life, such as diet. He felt she was doing okay, but also saw her take on an unhealthy peacekeeper role to avoid conflict between her parents. Volatility seemed to be the price for having both parents involved with her.

Ed's Journey

Ed had gathered many resources around him, which sustained, taught, and inspired him. "I might be the luckiest person in the world. Twenty years with a men's group, dear brothers. My new partner, Shelley, who walks on water and doesn't know it. And she likes *me*." Shelley had split from the father of her kids and since recreated a relationship with him, their kids, and his new wife. "There was a super hard time, but they made it through. The whole family is tight now. I don't know if it's possible for me, but I am hopeful."

New self-understanding from life coaching had improved his connection with Daphne. "I've seen my role in the dance that I couldn't see before, how I infuriated Daphne. When anything happened that wasn't cool, my default was to flee. As she got scarier, I would protect myself more and more by not telling her the truth. I'd save it for later, or lie. Now my relationship with her is off the boil." Having seen and taken responsibility for his part in past events, Ed could now make wiser choices.

As we wrapped up our interview, I asked what Ed would tell his earlier self. "It does get better. Time does some healing, there's a palpable difference in just a year. I cherish the quality that every second weekend offers. Charlene and I are focused and we have good times together."

And what else? "Take the money, stupid!"

The stressors here included Ed's efforts to get his business going, his avoidance of conflict, and his affair, not to mention Daphne's volatile temper, her ongoing depression, and her concussion symptoms. Ed built a strong set of supports for himself, and his growth gradually helped him grasp his role in the marriage problems. His relationship with Daphne was becoming smoother, though he could still see Charlene trying at times to be a peacekeeper. His girlfriend's example of close co-parenting gave Ed hope that he and Daphne could, in time, achieve the same thing.

What Does This Story Tell Us?

None of us knows what another is experiencing inside; we make educated guesses, ask, and make assumptions. What I appreciated about Ed's story is that he seemed to accept Daphne's struggles without a lot of judgment. That didn't mean he found them easy to live with, but he accepted their reality and coped as best he could, focusing on what he could do differently.

Ed described the impact of Daphne's depression and fiery temper on him and Charlene. Although the clashes were intense at times, Ed expanded his self-management skills to find new ways to respond, which improved his relationship with Daphne somewhat. Ed still saw their daughter taking a conciliatory role at times and wanted to change that. He felt optimistic about his influence on Charlene over time.

Ed also faced the same tasks as other co-parents: to deal with the ending of the marriage and build ways to share parenting. Fluctuations in mental health intensified the challenges, both for him and for Daphne. Ed didn't talk about what help Daphne was able to find. Generally, the impacts of conditions such as depression and concussions are becoming better understood. Because the co-parent's basic capacity to function is impacted, all systems around both parents — family, community, medical, educational — need to offer support in many ways.

7 Co-Parenting Children with Special Needs

No one really knows the best way to parent a child
with disabilities, so you have to make it up as you go.
— ALISON

As parents, we want our children to have the best life that they can. When they have a challenge, we want to help, to make it better. We must continually assess their needs and their progress, and accept where they are at that point — whether it's what we want for them or not. That key skill of accepting reality is needed again and again. We discern, accept, and act to meet each child's needs while keeping in mind other family members' requirements. This juggling ability is important particularly when children have long-term special needs.

The following stories stirred deep compassion and admiration in me. Alison needed to create a wide support network after she and Russell separated, leaving her with much of the parenting of their volatile child. Nolan's marriage with Pamela ended over differences in how to parent their autistic son and took a high-conflict turn. The needs of Jeannette's fairly low-functioning son changed as he matured, requiring determination and flexibility from those around him. From difficult starting points, facing gruelling demands, the parents found a way to nurture their children's growth and their own — and to keep going forward.

ALISON'S STORY:
MEETING HIGH DEMANDS

mental illness • isolation • growth

Forty-year-old Alison had an air of quiet competence. Dressed in jeans and a sweatshirt, she looked like clothes were well down her list of priorities. She was the first parent of a special needs child I interviewed, and the challenges she faced floored me. Although she had care of her eight-year-old daughter over 80 percent of the time, not meeting our definition of co-parenting, I have included her story because it feels so important.

"If you have a child with mental illness, behavioural issues, and explosive rages, divorce is that much harder. My daughter has spent time in the psych ward at the children's hospital. No parent wants to go through that, but you do, and you learn from it. Mika has a lot of special needs and it is highly demanding to parent her. I think we've done pretty well."

Alison and her husband, Russell, had adopted Mika when she was an infant. As Mika grew, Alison and Russell reacted differently to the challenges of parenting her. "I thought that the adoption was equal when we went into it, but he found the parenting overwhelming ... he didn't think of parenting in the same way that I did."

Mika was six when they separated, two years before our interview. "In the months before the split, I felt terrible, that this was on me. I did a lot of research on what children need. My ex was feeling surprised and angry about the split. At that sad time, it was not easy to talk about a parenting plan."

Fearing that Russell might opt out completely from parenting, Alison tried to persuade him that Mika would benefit from seeing both of her parents every week. Russell, though, wanted relatively little involvement. The parents had enough self-management skills to find a mediator and stay together for several extra months in order to make their decisions carefully. "We talked about every possibility, including the quickly discarded fantasy of a duplex in which our daughter could run back and forth between us." They eventually agreed that Mika would spend every other weekend with her dad, and they bought houses near each other.

Alison reflected on the huge challenge of parenting any child with special needs. "The divorce rate is higher for parents of children with special needs, across attention deficit disorder, autism, and other kinds of disabilities. It's unknown territory. No one knows the best way to parent a child with disabilities, so you have to make it up as you go along. In some ways, it was a relief when we split; I could just do things the way I think is best."

The First Years

Alison read up on a strategy to tell Mika about the coming split, where both parents sat down together to explain things. "Then one day Russell told Mika while they were driving to the Target store in the car, with no strategy whatsoever!" she said with exasperation. "That's not the way I would have done it, but I had to accept that it was done and move on. I was trying to be so conscientious."

Alison struggled to meet Mika's many needs. Her friends were great but could only help so much. Some didn't feel qualified or up to the challenge. "My daughter had explosive rages. At times I felt so tired, so completely done with Mika. I had nothing left to give. We hadn't worked out roles between Russell and me, so there was no one to hand off to. For a while, I felt I would never get settled into a new life."

They had to work out finances. "Russell felt I was destroying his life and plans for retirement by separating. I was trying to keep the focus on our daughter; he thought about money and financial stability. We made about the same income and we had been together for a long time, so it was clear we would divide costs equally. That made things easier."

Similar expectations about cost sharing formed a good foundation, but after the separation, Russell's financial decisions made him perennially short of money. This meant that Mika couldn't always take part in activities unless Alison contributed more. "Russell has made some bad choices. It's painful to watch, and when it affects Mika, I have to deal with the fallout."

Building Long-Term Supports

Alison spoke matter-of-factly. "It's isolating to parent a special needs child. You have to fight the teachers at school who think that you're part of the problem. You don't fit in with other parents whose problems with their kids are such small potatoes — they are important to them, but to me they're just gravy. So it's important to network with other parents, and sometimes that's hard to do. Parents, if they perceive that a child has issues, may steer their own child in another direction, to a child who may be easier to deal with. You really better have your own supports lined up."

Alison sought support from a parenting coach and found workshops on parenting special needs children. "It sucks to spend my weekends doing parenting workshops!" She joined a network of parents of special needs children and a divorce support group. "There's value in getting advice from others, and also in seeing the many ways that people handle things."

Alison appreciated every scrap of assistance offered, and could have used more. "I have a big support network — great friends who've been there for me. I recently bought a new house with a mother-in-law apartment. When friends visit us, they're right here and it's amazing." Her voice held wonder and longing at how manageable life felt during these visits.

Impacts on Mika

Alison and Russell had different parenting styles, with Russell placing fewer demands on Mika. Alison believed that Mika could adapt to different sets of rules, as long as those rules stayed constant. "Mika eats differently in the two houses; she has to code-switch from one home to the other. I think kids can do that."

Co-parenting changed Mika's relationship with her parents. Mika now spent lots of one-on-one time with them both, which she likes. Alison saw Mika worry about her father, blaming Alison for abandoning him. "I get to be the bad guy. I am the disciplinarian, the one making expectations of her."

On the other hand, Alison enjoyed much about her time with Mika. "I have a new and improved relationship with her now. She used to lavish all her love and affection on her dad. With him out of the picture, I get more of the good stuff — it feels more balanced and positive. A whole relationship."

As other parents observed, Alison saw a new breadth of experience for Mika. "Her dad and I are very different. Before, we did a narrow set of activities that we both enjoyed. She now gets opportunities to spend time with each of us, and worlds open up from that — two sets of leisure-time interests."

Navigating the Co-Parent Relationship

Alison acknowledged that her own behaviour caused flare-ups with Russell. "When I get tired and stressed, I may get more hostile and lash out in a way I don't normally. I will present my requests more like demands — that's not ever productive. I have my ups and downs, and so does he. I have such a range of emotions regarding him, from outrage to sympathy to pity to appreciation."

Having recently entered a new relationship, Alison wanted more nights off. "Mika freaks out if my new partner stays overnight. The two weekends a month with her dad aren't enough for me to develop a new relationship. I could use help from Russell, who hasn't shown any willingness to take her for a few extra nights a month. It's been frustrating. I don't know." She laughed with an edge of anger. "I'll find a way to get a few nights off, and it's better if she's with Russell than some random person."

From Survival to Acceptance and Interdependence

How did Alison deal with the ongoing stresses? "It varies. I complain to good friends and get sympathy and validation. Sometimes I try to discern whether my reaction is appropriate. And I decide whether to try to influence Russell, or not. Often I try to accept and move on."

Her world view expanded as she learned new skills. "Adversity does build character. I am more sympathetic toward others and able to support them. I have had to reach out for help more. I was an independent person before, and now I'm interdependent. It's better to be in a community; it can be isolating to be totally self-sufficient. To get there, though, you have to flex some new muscles. And for a while, you have to ask for help without being able to reciprocate. It's good to get to the other side of that, and be able to give back. In retrospect I wish I had asked for more help sooner. It would have been freely given, and we would have gotten back on our feet sooner."

Her perspectives had deepened. "I'm more curious about people. I work with folks who are pretty down and out. I didn't get, before, how challenges can present in people's lives and it not be their fault. I have a deeper understanding and a sincere interest in other people and their story ... more empathy and less judgment."

Her message to her earlier self: "I did lots of worrying and it didn't improve the outcomes! Relax a bit. Over time, things will get easier."

When Alison and Russell split, they had many things to sort out: how to parent Mika, how to meet Russell's wish for a smaller role in Mika's life, how to survive the isolating role of a parent of a special needs child — all while changing from one family to two. They took time to think through the transition and used a mediator. Their carefully crafted schedule gave Alison all except two weekends each month with Mika — a lot of time with a volatile child. Her parenting coach gave skillful help and Alison had social supports, but even so, she felt anxious and sometimes overwhelmed. By interview time, Alison had expanded her self-management skills. She could see her own contribution to conflicts with Russell, and had learned compassion for others and how to ask for help. Alison's growth helped her survive and sustained her in her new, bigger mothering role with Mika.

NOLAN'S STORY:
PARENTING DIFFERENCES AND COURT

autism • *high conflict* • *money*

"I had no idea what I was letting myself in for." Nolan, a fit, forty-four-year-old engineer, spoke as one used to being listened to. Nolan and

Pamela had divorced three years before Nolan's interview with me. Their son, Diego, now seven, had been diagnosed as high-functioning on the autism spectrum when he was two. The parents' different beliefs about what kind of parenting Diego needed sparked their divorce. Pamela's style with Diego was fairly relaxed, while Nolan used lots of structure. Nolan was blunt about the intensity of parenting Diego. "It's like parenting five ordinary children."

In the year leading up to the split, Pamela and Nolan took a course together on parenting children with special needs. Nolan hoped that they would be able to find common ground for parenting once they had received the same information. However, afterward Nolan saw little change in Pamela's parenting.

Nolan struggled with what to do. He had watched his own parents stay together, fighting constantly, until the children moved out. "I wished they had divorced. I thought maybe I could just stick with it in our marriage, but we weren't getting anywhere. It seemed better to do it when he was younger; she could parent her way, I could do it my way."

Nolan approached the split anticipating that he and Pamela would share parenting week-on/week-off. This way, Diego would receive the more structured support at home half of the time. Nolan's income was adequate to provide for all of them, or so he thought.

That's not how it turned out.

"I thought that fifty-fifty would be the norm. I know people who share parenting, and it's pretty effortless: they help each other out. My experience is the opposite. I was being completely honest, thinking we would split the assets and parenting time fifty-fifty. The level of animosity she showed was a complete surprise. She hired an aggressive lawyer who helped her to twist things in court. She even physically attacked me."

Nolan and Pamela went to two mediation sessions but made no progress, so litigation continued. The parents were now communicating only through email, by Nolan's choice. "We were both in a position where any email could be read out in future court cases. That kept things civil. If you have a pattern of being unreasonable, it's all there for a judge to see."

The judge's decisions covered both time and money. Nolan received less parenting time than he wanted. School holidays were split fifty-fifty, but the rest of the year he saw his son five weekdays and two weekends plus a few hours mid-week each month: almost 40 percent. Having less than 50 percent parenting time cost Nolan financially. "I've earned a lot of money. The judge reapportioned the assets so Pamela got 60 percent, I got 40 percent. My assets are gradually being drained in child and spousal support. I can't believe the legal system doesn't protect the father's basic right to spend time with the kids; the financial aspect is totally nuts. I find the law offensive."

Nolan found a way to manage his emotions. "In my head, I keep the financial side separate from the parenting. I've had to."

Supporting Diego's Personal Growth

Nolan found ways to shape Diego's behaviour in desirable directions, using repetition and concentrating on a few behaviours. "With these demanding behaviours, you have to persevere. You don't want to be authoritarian, but you can't be super soft, either. Diego always wanted sausage rolls when we were in the supermarket, and would throw a tantrum if he didn't get one. In my view, this came about because he did it the first time and got his way."

Nolan saw Diego reverting to his preferred patterns when with Pamela. "He would explode with anger unless we watched TV while eating supper. I got him out of that, but when I went away for ten days and returned, he was back in it. I knew it could be changed because I was doing it. But it takes a lot of persistence. Pamela liked to say, 'Ours is the fun house, there are no rules here.' I think it's confusing for him."

Years before, the parents had hired a coordinator to supervise Diego's personal education program. This decision had significant long-term benefits. The coordinator, still in place, set out a consistent set of rules for both homes, plus the school, to keep Diego on track. "That person has turned into a bit of an adjudicator, telling us what we should and shouldn't do. Diego was writing only in capital letters, and his mother wanted to let it go. The coordinator said we had to correct it every time or it wouldn't change. With autism, a lot of it is monitoring and recording behaviours, strategizing about how you will change them. The coordinator's independent advice has been very helpful."

Regardless of the battles with Pamela, Nolan felt good about his relationship with his son. "Diego's not aware of most of the conflicts. I see him a lot and I am better than just a weekend dad. I've had great vacations with him. We have the cute stuff, cuddling in bed with a story, with him telling me he loves me. I've been teaching Diego to tie his shoelaces — he just forgets. I have a strong relationship with him."

Nolan also felt content about the array of people around Diego. "He has a number of supports besides me: a therapist he really likes; his mom; her boyfriend, whom he likes; my partner; and a long-term babysitter he loves."

Nolan had adjusted to enduring sustained hostility from Pamela. "The level of anger is the hardest thing to deal with. I've learned to let go of my frustration by thinking about it rationally. What are you going to do? I could obsess about it, get drunk every night, let it wreck my life. I thought about walking away, but I have a responsibility to my son that's more important than anything. Since I have to live with it, there isn't really a lot of choice." Nolan's laugh had jagged edges.

Supports for Nolan

Those around him enabled Nolan to survive the intensity and not feel alone. "It helps to have people to talk to about things. You don't want to always be banging on about it, but they understand what's going on. I saw a counsellor for two years — that was good. He may have helped me let go of my anger a bit. He had some good suggestions, like the parenting course before we split up. Talking with him was grounding. He said he had counselled hundreds of couples and what I was going through wasn't normal, was at the extreme end. It was a validation."

The ongoing legal battles had impacted those around Nolan, too. "My family has been great, but it's hard for them to understand. They get more upset than I do. My new partner's been terrific in the last year. Stepping into my life is not easy, and it's driven pretty well everyone else away."

By the interview's end, Nolan sounded reconciled to his situation. "There's a constant evolution as my son gets older. I'm still the same person I was, but you get tested in different ways. I see him almost 40 percent of the time. A lot of people have it a lot worse."

What would he say to an earlier Nolan? "I wouldn't say I regret it, but I had no idea how difficult it would be. I wouldn't recommend this for anyone else, but assume the worst motivation for all the nice stuff. Assume you have someone who wants to go for the jugular. It's sad that it couldn't have been amicable."

Stressors intensify any differences between couples, and Diego's special needs accentuated the divergent parenting approaches of his father and mother. Nolan's leaving produced a highly and unexpectedly aggressive response from Pamela. Nolan felt blindsided and then run over by the legal system. He sought helpful resources for himself and for Diego, which his financial health allowed him to obtain. His self-management skills allowed him to accept, in time, the level of Pamela's hostility. Nolan didn't feel that he had changed much, except for learning to survive unexpected aggression. He also had lost all trust in the legal system.

Two positive results stood out amid all the struggles between Nolan and Pamela. Most importantly, Diego enjoyed a close relationship with both his parents — a worthwhile accomplishment. In addition, the parents' continued use of Diego's program coordinator gave Diego's life helpful coherence and consistency. For me, these elements redeemed a story of stark and sustained discord.

JEANNETTE'S STORY: BALANCING NEEDS

severe autism • shifting arrangements decision-making

Jeannette spoke with me fourteen years after her divorce; her daughter was then seventeen, her son, nineteen. Her son's diagnosis of autism when he was four had triggered big changes. "I was so unaware; I saw myself only as others perceived me. I didn't realize that our marriage wasn't meeting my needs. The diagnosis of autism caused me to look at my life under a microscope, and I quickly saw that it wasn't working.

We tried to fix things with counselling, but it didn't help. It was time to move on."

Her daughter, Serena, was three and her son, Ben, was five when Jeannette and Al divorced. Jeannette had read a lot about special needs children and the importance of consistency for them. Knowing that she needed to leave for her own peace of mind, she moved into a new place, trusting that Ben would get used to the different setting. "That was liberating for me. Despite all the experts saying that change is bad for special needs kids, I think change is only bad if you make it that way. Ben was able to make the adjustment."

Parenting time and living arrangements shifted repeatedly in the fourteen years following the divorce. Jeannette made early decisions based on her lawyer's advice, some of which she later regretted. "Initially, I had both kids all the time except for one night each week. Until then, Al hadn't had much involvement with them; when I told my three-year-old that Daddy wouldn't be living with us anymore, she said, 'Daddy doesn't live with us now, he lives at work.'" Al gradually became more involved. Three years later, he had the children 30 percent of the time. Jeannette wasn't enthusiastic. "While I didn't want to deny him his children, I didn't feel that he was the best influence for them. He wanted 50 percent, so thirty was a huge compromise for him."

When Jeannette remarried, her new family encountered choppy water. "Especially in a remarriage, having a special needs child is a huge stressor. Ben's severe autism meant that as he grew, he became increasingly strong and unpredictable. My [second] husband made it through rough times when Ben was smearing poop everywhere, when he was hurting my new husband's children — it's an amazing thing that he made it through. This was the hardest thing in our marriage." When Jeannette had another baby, she had to be vigilant all the time, never knowing if Ben would blow up or cuddle. "I had a meltdown, crying, 'I can't do this, I can't keep anybody safe.' I was a weeping mess. My husband was so great, to be concerned for all of us and take it in stride."

As Ben grew stronger physically, Jeannette learned to steel herself in order to accept the situation and not be overwhelmed by her feelings. "Ben's never been easy, but when he hit age eleven, he got larger and his violent outbursts were no longer controllable by one person. It took two people to keep others safe from him." In one three-month period, the school called her fifty-two times to come and get Ben because he was acting out. Sometimes the teachers didn't feel Jeannette would be safe having Ben in the car with her when she picked him up. "Ninety percent of the time he's fine; it's just the 10 percent he's unpredictable."

Jeannette and Al didn't agree on how to respond to Ben's changing needs. Al didn't want him to be medicated. Jeannette said, "If you aren't okay with medication for him, then you will need to live with him, because I can't." Al took over primary custody of Ben, providing two caregivers who were with Ben most of the time. Jeannette now saw Ben every other weekend. "This arrangement has been a nice break for us. Serena is with me; her schedule stayed the same. She stays with me and visits her dad, just as before."

Hasty Decisions and an Uneasy Balance of Power

While Ben's autism brought unusual stresses, Jeannette's feelings about the legal system echoed many other parents'. She regretted her early legal steps, done in haste. "My first lawyer led me to believe that anything you sign can be easily changed. My second lawyer, who was much better, showed me that the status quo had a lot of power."

Jeannette had wanted to have the divorce over with quickly, and now wished she had made decisions more slowly to ensure that things were right. She had prioritized time with the children and didn't want to hassle over money. "I didn't understand that one factor could impact the other. Now Al gets what he wants because he has deep pockets for lawyers and I don't. I didn't see that I might need that money to fight and advocate for the kids."

She regretted not having had a guide or resource to help her make wise decisions. "It's harder to leave a marriage than to get married. I didn't find any books that talked about how to make decisions or said that the status quo is important. A guideline would have been great on how to choose a mediator, and how to decide if you will use a mediator."

Stretching to Meet Many Needs

"My personal growth kicked off with the divorce and hasn't stopped." As a mother of a special needs child, Jeannette initially found little help available. "No one in my family had been divorced before me. My parents were understandably overwhelmed by my son. Even if I said, 'I need you to come and do this thing,' they wouldn't. I didn't feel I had support until I remarried."

She created a circle to sustain her. "There were no local support groups, so I started one. My support came from helping others. I found a lot of help communicating on day-to-day issues with other special needs mothers."

She also found help further afield. "I tried counselling and ended up going to a program in the U.S., which has workshops on special needs kids and also on personal growth. I would never have found a place like this without Ben's situation. At first it felt like a cult, but I stayed because I thought it would help Ben. It was so powerful. I kept going back, and learned about myself and being happy and feeling empowered. I think I was on that path as a child and lost it as a young adult."

Jeannette could see how her behaviour had changed. She used to get upset during conflict. "Now I try to ask why this is upsetting me, instead of just letting anger sit in the pit of my stomach. I've learned to stop and process things before I fly off the handle. Because I have learned what pushes my buttons, I am triggered less often. Physical movement always helps, too."

Once she began reaching out for help, she developed an ever-growing community. "People who worked with Ben quickly became part of a large extended family ... they stay in our lives when they're done. So I have this huge, amazing group of people who have spent time with my son and my family."

Current Equilibrium

After fourteen years of co-parenting, Jeannette still didn't feel that she and Al had a final parenting agreement. "We agree on the amount of time with each of us and then create flexibility, mainly around Al's work schedule. Then he still wants to change it. The differences that made you divorce don't disappear! I am in an endless negotiation with him. I don't like conflict, but I know that it will always be there. If it's going to be a big fight, it will involve lawyers."

Her situation with both children had become more manageable. "The family that lives with me is getting a chance to exhale. Serena's a really good kid, the kind that everyone wants to have. It's nice to know she feels grounded living with the healthy relationship between me and my current husband."

Jeannette still felt discomfort about Serena's relationship with her father. "When she's at his house for any period of time, she calls me at least twelve times a day, wanting to feel connected. When we talked about her learning to ride the bus, her first comment was, 'Then I can come to your house more!'" Serena had said she would rather not go to her father's at all.

Jeannette believed that Ben was getting his needs met. "At his level of functioning, which is quite low, he has shelter, food, and something to do. He will likely be equally happy or unhappy wherever he is. When he sees me, he's happy to see me, and it doesn't matter if he hasn't seen me for a day or a week, he's simply glad to see me. It's kind of a relief. This custody schedule is giving my family a break from an exhausting time with someone who can become violent and scary. I can be comfortable knowing that he's not over there missing me."

Jeannette worked hard to learn about Ben's condition and needs, and to meet them. His behaviour strongly impacted the rest of the family; in time, even their physical safety. The parents' different values emerged as they tried to balance Ben's needs with those of other family members. Good financial health allowed Al the option of hiring more caregivers, and he took Ben full-time three years before our interview. In the face of extraordinary ongoing stresses, Jeannette's growth allowed her to keep going, navigate conflicts with Al, and find solutions for her children and herself.

What Do These Stories Tell Us?

Alison, Nolan, and Jeannette described the intense and sustained demands of co-parenting a child with special needs. Those needs seemed to be on a different scale than those of children in previous stories, requiring deep commitment and effort. More challenges arose as parents dealt with their co-parent's differing ways of nurturing their special needs child. Alison, Nolan, and Jeannette learned to accept that they would need help, and how to reach out for it. Each found ways to deal with their strong, sometimes overpowering, emotions.

Meeting larger special needs required more resources, both human and financial. Nolan's and Jeannette's stories particularly showed how financial health expanded parents' options. Lots of support, some of it expensive, helped greatly, but they still faced hurdles. The parents' self-management skills and determination allowed them to keep creating new ways forward. The courage threaded through their stories, as well as in those in the following chapter, humbled me.

8 Feelings from the Past: Regrets, Choices, and Guilt

I don't know if I'm supposed to be holding on or letting go.
— UNKNOWN

Each co-parenting story is two tales intertwined: the ending of a marriage, and the rebuilding of lives as two new families. While separate, they interweave closely. Grappling with the loss and pain of the marriage breakdown is vital to successful co-parenting.

How do we deal with loss? By letting ourselves mourn. Co-parenting is an evolution in which grieving is key. I think of grieving as a time of snipping our many emotional ties inside. Each time a connection to the other person comes up in our hearts or minds, we have to feel it, cut it, and let it go. Each snip hurts.

The rate of progress through grief is often different within a couple. By the time one partner has decided they want to leave and tells the other, that first person will have privately cut many emotional ties. The other partner may be far behind in their own sadness and letting go.

Only when a partner believes they can survive without the other person can they move into a new future. Without that confidence, the person being left can cling with frantic force to their former spouse.

In the stories that follow, feelings from the past seemed not to be resolved or accepted. Shannon's core inability to accept her divorce impacted her and her children. Jeff's life as a divorced dad was shadowed by guilt for many years. Jocelyne found that one early decision she made had wider impacts than she could've imagined, and she struggled with regret for years. Ripples of pain remained that could not be stilled.

SHANNON'S STORY:
IF ONLY

holding on to past ties

Shannon was a thirtyish, slightly built woman with long brown hair. Soft-spoken, she appeared positive and determined, yet seemed not to take up much space in the room. The difference between the life she wanted and the one she got lay below all her words. After a first separation of one year, she and her husband, David, had reconnected, sharing a home for four years more with their two daughters. During these years, they lived together but led separate emotional lives.

Shannon knew things weren't good in the last four years together with David, but she didn't know what to do. "The kids and I did outings all the time. It was fun. I had mornings with them, he had evenings. He would disappear for periods of time, and I just ignored it. I didn't ask where he had been. I didn't think I could be a single mother, I get too anxious. So, for years, when David would talk about divorce I'd say, 'If we divorce, you take the children.' That kept us from splitting."

The First Years Separated

When they finally separated, their daughters were five and eight years old. Shannon's world changed. "I envisaged dividing assets equally and getting child support, but it never happened." It was not clear why she received so little financially from the divorce. One cause may have been her unwillingness to engage in the process. "Partly, I didn't get a lawyer because I wanted to avoid the adversarial legal system. I was expecting to be able to buy a house close to the girls' school; I never expected not to get anything at all!" The lack of money took a huge toll on her and her ability to provide for her children. With no capital assets, Shannon couldn't consider buying a house, and had stayed in rental accommodation ever since.

Lack of money led to sustained stress. "I had to move six times during the first two years post-separation. So much upheaval! I hadn't any attention for mothering, between moving and having to go to court. I was able to go on a few school trips with the girls, and they had their friends over, after school." The girls spent several days each week with Shannon and the rest with their father.

Shannon had an air of bewildered disappointment. She didn't express anger, but rather seemed to be looking around her, wondering how she had ended up here. She blamed the system for not saving the marriage. "If those social services had been more proactive in counselling, then we would have been okay. The family counsellor didn't help us address our issues; it was more about moving to separate lives. I wish I had gone to the Employee Assistance Program,* but I was afraid to go because my friend had gone and was told to get a divorce. The system let me and my family down." Her implied message: "The divorce should *not* have happened."

Shannon had been diligent in accessing various supports. She found a mediator for herself and her husband, then later a community group for divorced parents, and sought counselling for herself. "I thought I was going crazy. The counsellor told me I didn't seem crazy. The whole process caused me to relive the losses of my childhood, when my parents divorced." Revisiting deprivations from her past seemed to have amplified her current pain and may have made it seem too big to handle. Sadness flowed from her for what might have been.

Her goal in co-parenting was to give the children a balanced life. "The best of both is what I wanted — their father's materialism and my own more inner and spiritually oriented life."

Ripples Persisting: Impacts

Six years past the separation, Shannon held a steady administrative job, which allowed her to rent a small apartment fairly near her ex's house. Her daughters had been living mainly with their father, seeing Shannon

---

*The Employee Assistance Program is aimed at aiding with issues that may be affecting job performance, including counselling about family dynamics and possible separation.

overnight once or twice a week. She had taken training in communications skills and public speaking, and joined community groups protecting the environment.

Shannon felt the children were getting a good blend of herself and David. "They have been able to stay in this community, with the same church and circle of friends. I thought they were getting the best of both parents." She saw David and herself as very different influences. "The girls have been getting two polarized perspectives of the world. Of diet — healthy or unhealthy. Of how one spends leisure time — constructive or destructive. Of how one balances the body, mind, and heart. I want to turn their minds to a wholesome perspective of everything they choose to do. My husband is more about absorbing and responding. It's two different worlds." The only exceptions to the black-and-white view of David versus herself came in her acknowledgement that her children had better social status through their father. They also had video games and online connections with friends at his place, which she couldn't offer.

Two months before our interview, things had changed. Both girls told her they wanted to live with their father full-time.

Shannon reported this shift calmly; if she grieved losing time with her children, she did not express it. Since then, she said she had been able to lead a more balanced life. She felt more able to contribute to her children's lives at a community level rather than an individual level. "I don't see the kids as mine anymore; they are little spiritual beings on loan. I did need to micromanage their lives until they were seven. Now I secure their future by helping out with climate change and initiatives to protect the environment."

For herself, Shannon focused on finding inner peace. "I still have struggles with that. I've taken a Toastmasters program and a meditation course to help me with this. I feel like the divorce has stolen my peace and I am still trying to find it." Shannon still referred to David as her husband, a signal that she had not accepted the end of her marriage.

Heaviness from this interview stayed with me. Much of Shannon's energy seemed to be occupied with the feeling that, "This is wrong." The lopsided financial outcome seemed unfair, having severely limited Shannon's options. These issues had cost both Shannon and her children.

Her daughters' choice to live full-time with their father showed that something wasn't working for them in their time with her, yet Shannon appeared unaffected. I didn't understand that, but I admired Shannon's courage to keep going and explore new paths. She found a global cause, the environment, which helped give meaning to her life. It did not, though, provide the peace she sought for herself. Shannon's inability to accept reality — the loss of her marriage — impacted everything she did. It acted like an anchor, holding her back from fully participating in her new life.

JEFF'S STORY:
SLOW JOURNEY THROUGH GUILT

> *guilt • family history*
> *holding feelings inside*

A sandy-haired union steward with a soft, intense voice, Jeff met with me fifteen years after he and his former wife, Rhea, had separated. Jeff had stayed in his unhappy marriage until his son, Simon, was six, because the thought of leaving filled him with guilt. His own father had left the family when Jeff was young, and he didn't want to repeat his dad's mistakes. Jeff had already tried separating, moving to his parents' basement, but returned after a month, full of remorse. The couple tried mediation but made little progress. One year later, Jeff left for good, unwilling to let his son experience a loveless relationship between his parents.

Young Simon didn't want his father to go. Jeff remembered his painful leaving day. "I was trying to open the drawers of the dresser to pack. Simon was holding onto the drawer with his fingers as hard as he could so I couldn't pull it out to empty it."

Jeff felt so guilty after making the break that he wanted Rhea to have the house and most of the furniture; he felt this would minimize the impact of the separation on Simon. For the first six months, he arranged for his paycheque to go directly to Rhea, and she gave him an allowance.

Then he decided that was going too far. "I had my cheque brought back to me, and forwarded money to her."

The couple held different expectations of marriage and divorce. Jeff saw Rhea assuming that parents would always be together, whether the marriage was good or bad. Her immense anger at Jeff for holding another view lasted several years post-divorce.

Rhea served Jeff with divorce papers, and they discussed when Jeff would see Simon. "She wanted me to have him all weekends. She also saw that flexibility was best for everyone. I tried hard to leave my ego at the door in our discussions. No matter how much animosity I felt, I needed to focus on my son's needs and the impacts on him."

For the first three years, Jeff saw Simon after school several nights each week, and had him each weekend. He and Rhea jointly attended parent-teacher meetings and Simon's hockey games. After three years, he was able to buy a house nearby, and Simon's time became more equally divided.

Though he tried to keep things smooth, Jeff encountered rocky patches. When Simon was in second grade, his guidance counsellor met with both parents to tell them that Simon had been assessed with a low IQ. Rhea told Jeff she held him responsible. "We walked back to her house, with her blaming me. She went in and shut the door, with me standing on the step, crying." His face tightened with remembered pain. Fortunately, in later years Rhea realized that Jeff was still a decent parent, and their relationship improved.

Jeff's Journey

Jeff received a lot of support from his mother and stepfather, who were the only people he told about his divorce. Jeff mostly kept his struggles to himself. He knew a few other people going through divorce, but was wary of sharing. "I didn't talk to others — there's a trust factor, it's private." Jeff's feelings of guilt and perhaps shame prevented him from telling others what he was going through. This meant that the same thoughts and feelings kept whirling around in his head, with few other perspectives to offer relief or a way forward.

Jeff's life post-separation included going out with women and spending lots of time with Simon. Jeff didn't show awareness, generally, of other choices he could have made in co-parenting, but he confided that he had probably started dating too soon. "I masked my guilt by dating other women. I would have been better to wait and get to know myself better before entering into other relationships. You have to separate on your time — be prepared mentally and emotionally."

Jeff felt bad for being separated from Simon. "I called my son every night to say 'I love you,' but I wasn't there." Yet Simon still benefited. "He got to see both parents as they want to be as parents, without any influence from the ex-partner. He got relaxed time with each of us. He saw that Mom and Dad could work together, how both of our personalities came out in our love for him. He got time with grandparents, too." Rhea's anger abated enough to allow a sorting-through of finances and discussion of co-parenting.

Jeff paid a long price for leaving his marriage. His childhood experience of his father's leaving the family made it hard for him to accept his own decision to leave Rhea. His lack of acceptance led to guilt, which made him take on whatever blame and criticism Rhea aimed at him. He entered the dating world quickly to distract himself from his feelings, but recognized later that he wasn't ready; he lacked self-understanding and self-acceptance.

This kind man seemed to have stayed longer in the land of worry and regret than he might have if he had found help to work through his feelings. Many people seek support or somewhere to share their story. Jeff's choice to confide only in his parents, keeping much of his guilt and worry gripped tightly inside, allowed those feelings to control him for many years. Talking with a counsellor or a peer group may have helped him accept his decision to separate and live less weighed down by guilt. Jeff did eventually accept his choices and his feelings. He built his new life, taking joy in Simon's growing maturity. It just took more time.

JOCELYNE'S STORY:
A DECISION REGRETTED

distance parenting • abrupt changes • regrets

Jocelyne, a wiry accountant in her fifties, gripped her arms against her body as she quietly told her story. Her geographical separation from her children lasted only one year, but that separation's impacts continued for decades.

She and her husband, Mike, separated in 1984, after ten years of marriage. At the time, their daughter, Sandra, was four and son, Nathan, six. They lived in Winnipeg. With two parents working full-time, life was busy.

Jocelyne was caught totally unprepared when Mike told her he wanted a separation. "There was a lot of discussion and disagreement. I wanted Mike to leave the house and he wanted me to leave; I wanted to keep the kids and so did he." Feeling that she couldn't afford to keep the kids full-time, Jocelyne agreed to have them from Friday night to Sunday night. Her capitulation wasn't only based on finances. A vague inner feeling also influenced her. "It wasn't just that I couldn't afford custody; I didn't feel I deserved it."

The pair shared parenting for a year. Jocelyne recalled, "I didn't go out on weekends — I was happy to have the kids all day. We could do stuff during the day and cuddle in the evenings. Weekdays, I could work as long as I needed to and then go home. I felt like my metabolism was always up — I felt a level of stress, to make sure I could always be there." She focused fully on her kids every weekend, partly for love of them and partly because she didn't have many close friends. "I had always felt that my romantic partner would be everything to me."

The kids coped pretty well with the weekdays/weekend schedule. Then, when the divorce became final in 1986, everything changed. When Jocelyne arrived at Mike's house one Friday evening, new owners answered the door. Mike had moved with the children to Edmonton, where he had a new job. He callously had given Jocelyne no indication or notice. "I was shocked, devastated. I couldn't believe he would do that to me, to us!"

Within a week, Jocelyne had tracked Mike down and had an agonizing conversation. If she wanted to see the kids, she would have to move to Edmonton. Halfway through a two-year accounting program, she wrestled with what to do. She hired a lawyer, who said it wasn't worth attempting legal action. Finally, she chose to stay in Winnipeg for the year it would take her to finish her training. She came to regret that decision.

During that year of separation, Jocelyne flew to Edmonton for weekends whenever she could afford to. As soon as her training finished, she moved to Edmonton, where she was again on the weekend schedule, picking up the kids on Friday nights. They were now seven and nine.

She sensed that her children very much needed what she offered them. "It seemed to me that Mike was seldom with them. Clearly, they were making a lot of their own food, and sometimes their sheets stank. I would get their stuff together and gather them into the car. They'd be so hyper, shouting 'Mommy! Mommy!' It would take me hours to bring them down. We'd get to my place and I would get them into the bath and pajamas, and we would cuddle. By Saturday afternoon, they would be calmed down and have unloaded about their week. It made me so happy that I could contribute to them, really do something for them."

This equilibrium lasted until their teen years. "Later, as they were older, they didn't necessarily want to come to my place. And Mike told me I could have them only every second weekend. I argued, but he stuck to that. My lawyer told me I had no recourse, as Mike was the custodial parent. I was angry then; but now, thinking that the kids likely had their own friends at his place, perhaps that was best for them."

Although her children were adults when we spoke, Jocelyne's choice to be separated for that one year haunted her even now. "I have huge regrets — I still blame myself." Tears leaked down her cheeks. "My son and I are on good terms, but my daughter still blames me, saying I abandoned her." Jocelyne and Sandra were not currently on speaking terms. "All these years I've blamed myself. My guilt over having left them is still raw."

Jocelyne's Personal Growth

For many years, books and professional training met Jocelyne's thirst for learning. She went back to school twice and advanced in her career. She also began to feel more confidence in herself. "I learned I wasn't stupid — Mike had told me I was." She loved reading. "I think I've been saved by some of my books."

Recently, she had gone beyond reading and taken personal-growth workshops. "Last year I decided I was going to forgive myself, and I am working on it. I am not sure I have been successful yet." She found it gruelling at times, but her life perspective was shifting. "I see that the kids have grown up okay, they're not drug addicts. Some of the things I've tried to instill in them are there. I'm proud of them." Her burden of regret was growing lighter.

Mike's unexpected relocation of the children forced Jocelyne to choose between finishing her professional training and seeing her children every weekend. Though she had made the best decision she could, pain from the year's separation weighed her down for decades. Jocelyne only began to develop a broader view of her life when she attended workshops on self-growth and forgiveness. Learning to accept herself and her decisions — a key part of her reality — allowed hope to sprout. Self-forgiveness brought feelings of peace and optimism that her relationship with Sandra could improve.

What Do These Stories Tell Us?

If we are lucky, when a loss occurs we feel its impact. Perhaps we are laid low for a period of time, and then slowly, gradually, we absorb the hurt and move past it. It has changed us but has subsided into the background. Our feelings from it are triggered only occasionally.

For Shannon, Jeff, and Jocelyne, the unaccepted losses associated with divorce stayed with them, like an anchor dragging on their energy and attention. Shannon stayed stuck, convinced that the divorce shouldn't have happened. Feelings remaining from her parents' divorce may have made her own more difficult to accept. Jeff carried his pain and guilt for many years. He shared some of his experiences with his parents, which helped him somewhat.* Jocelyne found solace in books, beginning to shed the weight of regret when she enrolled in live courses on personal growth. When Jeff and Jocelyne were able, finally, to accept their personal realities, their burdens began to dissolve. They lived more freely.

Accepting reality, one of the self-management skills from Chapter 2, is critical. We must make this inner shift before we can wholeheartedly take action in our outer world.

---

*While speaking our experience to any safe person can heal, choosing people with a different or broader perspective than our own can be particularly helpful.

9 Lesbian Couples: Co-Parenting with Two Mothers

When we least expect it, life sets us a challenge
to test our courage and willingness to change.
— PAULO COELHO

At the risk of stating the obvious, becoming a parent is more complicated for same-sex couples than for heterosexual folks. By necessity, a third party is involved.

Daily parenting and co-parenting are also complicated by the dominant social presumption that parents will be one male and one female. There are things to consider and attend to that heterosexual parents take for granted. The education system, for instance. Does the child's school offer a variety of images of families so the child will feel included? Do the co-parents get a relaxed welcome at parent-teacher meetings and school events?

Legally, things are different, too. Many jurisdictions have not recognized same-sex marriages. The stories here contain weddings or commitment ceremonies that may have included religious aspects but lacked legal status.* Couples publicly celebrated their unions with deeply cherished ceremonies while knowing they were not considered married in the eyes of the law. Ceremonies were typically called "weddings" and their dissolution "divorces" regardless of the legalities.

---

*I couldn't find any gay men co-parenting to interview, so their stories are absent.

Ironically, the inability of these couples to marry legally, which they desired at the time of their wedding or commitment ceremony, simplified their separation. In law, no marriage had occurred. Couples were free to determine how they would deconstruct their family without any reference to the courts. Not all co-parents found this freedom advantageous, as shown below.

All three mothers in the following stories had fairly high self-management skills. Marian's grief over separating from Beth was overwhelming at first; with time and growth, she and Beth co-operated fully in parenting their daughter. Elaine needed to reconstruct both her work and personal life after her separation. She sought supports and found that her growth helped her talk with her children as they made sense of the divorce. Wanda faced the challenge of co-parenting as the "second mother" when her original partner married a man.

MARIAN'S STORY:
KEEPING THE FOCUS ON THE CHILD

adoption • shared focus • low conflict

"We kept our daughter's needs front and centre," said Marian, a self-contained, articulate fifty-year-old with a direct gaze and quiet hands.

Her daughter, Wyn, was eleven when we spoke. Marian and her partner, Beth, had separated when Wyn was two.

Marian's composure anchored a story with remarkably low friction between the parents and a clear focus on their daughter. Marian and Beth had been together fifteen years and were both in their forties when they adopted Wyn. Marian said, "Anger was never my go-to reaction. More often I'd get sad."

Years of trying to get pregnant intensified Marian's yearning to be a family. They tried in vitro fertilization, an uncomfortable and invasive procedure, for eight years. "Once we decided to adopt, it was like going down a slide — so smooth, we both felt this was the child we were meant to have." Her eyes gleamed. "We were able to be at her birth."

Regret tinged Marian's voice. "When you have a child, something has to give in how you spend time. Couple time is what went in our house. I was focused on Wyn, and Beth felt lonely. She ended up forming another emotional attachment and felt she needed to leave. We went to couples therapy, but Beth had already fallen in love with someone else." The therapy helped Marian understand her part in the relationship breakdown, so she didn't heap blame on Beth.

The first phase of separating was lonely and painful. "I remember lying on the floor, crying, with Beth on one side of me and Wyn on the other, patting me on the shoulder, trying to help me. I felt sad and weak. The beauty of having a toddler is that you can't just stay in bed, you have to get up!"

Marian suffered, yet the breakup held little blame and anger. Both were gripped by strong feelings: Marian was grieving and Beth felt guilty. They negotiated their schedule without needing to protect themselves or trying to hurt the other parent, and they were able to keep the focus on Wyn. "We didn't fight, and we committed to not criticizing each other. Even when we were together, it was never a relationship with fighting." Because of Marian's and Beth's self-management skills, Wyn didn't hear one mother criticizing the other.

Marian and Beth's separation was simple because they had been unable to wed legally. "We set up an agreement, and talked dollars. As I had more assets, I'd pay 60 percent. We've kept a pretty loose arrangement — if one of us feels strongly about something, we pay for that."

Interdependent Co-Parenting

Marian sought books and articles to help them make good joint decisions and parent together. She liked *Mom's House, Dad's House: Making Two Homes for Your Child*, which talked about children's growth and what they need from their parents at each stage. It said that at two years old, a child needs to see both parents every day.

Marian knew she needed Beth. "I wanted to be able to rely on her as my parenting partner; it was too hard for me alone. I understood that our schedule needed to work for both of us so I could get my needs met. It wasn't a control thing, or us trying to hurt each other."

Their schedule evolved with time. Marian stayed in their house. Her work as a writer gave her flexibility, so she initially spent more time with Wyn. Beth moved into a rental and then into a house with her new girl-friend. At first, Wyn spent five nights a week with Marian and two nights a week with Beth. Two years later, they shifted to four nights and three nights — Monday, Wednesday, and Friday with Beth, and with Marian the other nights.

Marian and Beth tried to have the same rules in their houses so Wyn wouldn't have to reconcile two different worlds. They found houses close to each other so their daughter could walk back and forth between them. Marian felt lucky that their finances let them live with school and friends all within a few blocks.

Marian had more faith in her ex's parenting skills than in her own, something rarely heard in these interviews. She felt herself too lax. "I wish I could be the kind, thoughtful disciplinarian who lets natural consequences happen. It's at Beth's house where homework, chores, and manners are addressed."

Overall, the parents' respect for each other continued and their co-operation evolved. They celebrated Wyn's birthday together, and the parents and new partners plus Wyn were now taking some vacations jointly. "We love each other still; it's more like sisters now."

Impacts on Wyn

Marian saw Wyn benefit from co-parenting through lots of one-on-one time with a parent who was fresh. Wyn was never dragged around the grocery store hungry and tired, as a child of a single parent or a child with siblings might be. Her needs always came first. On the other hand, Marian thought Wyn might be getting too much attention focused on her and wanted to teach Wyn more empathy.

Marian's Journey

"In the early days, it hurt to see Beth. How do you parent when the life is being sucked out of you by seeing your ex?" Wyn helped Marian survive. "Toddlers are so in the moment, you have to be with them where they are. They are demanding, but what they ask you is usually interesting, and you can get through it if you stay in the present. I knew I would only do parenting for twenty-four hours at a time, so I could hang in with whatever she would bring."

Marian's family lived two thousand miles away, so although they phoned her often, she needed local supports. Church friends and her counsellor became particularly important. "That therapist saved my life. I was very depressed after we split, I felt like a failure. Having the therapist, and a toddler to care for, kept me going."

She learned to live on her own. She discovered she could live by herself and take care of things, and she enjoyed her own company. Marian valued how co-parenting supported her health and growth. She always had time for herself and her pursuits, with at least two nights a week to go out or take a class. She brought fresh insights and ideas into her time with Wyn. "Even with lots of support, parenting is really hard. I would wish that every parent has time to themselves."

Even with all of Marian's growth and adjustments, costs remained. "We both care about our daughter, but we aren't partners. I miss having a life partner who is my parenting partner. Every day it's hard not to have someone to laugh with."

Marian emphasized the importance of self-management skills in a partner. "When you decide to be a parent, choose wisely — a mature, big-hearted, kind, flexible person. Someone you can work with, whether you are in love with them or not. Those are the most important things, and I still have that in my ex-partner." So true, and perhaps hard to remember when our hormones are dancing the tango!

Marian's ten-year struggle to become pregnant before Wyn's adoption made her value her family intensely. Its loss, when Beth formed a new attachment outside the marriage, was wrenching, and Marian struggled with living on her own. Fortunately, Marian and Beth had good financial and physical health, as well as similar expectations of co-parenting. They avoided open conflict, showing much self-awareness and willingness to take others' needs into account — key self-management skills. They shared parenting smoothly, to Wyn's benefit.

ELAINE'S STORY:
KEEPING HER HEAD ABOVE WATER

talking with the children
seeking support • growth

When her partner left, Elaine felt like she was drowning. Elaine and her ex, Greta, had shared a landscape design business, as well as being parents and spouses, so their separation meant home, parenting, business, and finances all needed reshaping. "I fell through a sinkhole. The kids needing me was the only thing that kept my head above water."

Elaine's growth not only enabled her survival, but increased her ability to give her sons what they needed.

While unable to legally marry, Elaine and Greta had shared a joyful wedding ceremony ten years before. Elaine and I talked two years after Greta had moved out. Fifty years old, Elaine was still early in co-parenting her five- and eight-year-old sons, Gavin and Stefan. She moved lightly and powerfully around her living room as we spoke.

In her first months, she felt incompetent, thrown suddenly into chaos she hadn't chosen. "I was constantly trying to regulate my own emotions and figure out what the implications might be for the boys. Huge waves of feelings around little things, like how to pay an overdue gas bill. I'd need to sort it out with the company and get Greta to transfer the bill to me. Every mundane task had an emotional toll."

Her life felt scrambled. They had no process for dividing possessions, and Greta often dropped in to pick things up. Elaine never knew what might be gone next from the house.

Her sons kept her going. "Every day I woke up and had to figure out what the boys would need that day. Without them, I would have wanted to send my resignation in, to whomever I could find. But I couldn't, because their lives had to go on as cleanly as possible."

Feeling isolated and overwhelmed, Elaine sought counsel from two specialized therapists. Both said that consistency of the kids' schedules was key, so she focused on minimizing disruption. The mothers did hand-offs through the school. Either the boys had everything with them or one parent would drop it off at the other's house.

Making Co-Parenting Work

Elaine stayed in the family home and Greta found a place near the kids' school. Because the parents saw scheduling differently, they had to talk it through. Greta wanted to have the children week-on/week-off so she could travel for business. Elaine wanted more frequent contact, feeling that the boys needed to see them both every week. To reach an agreement, Elaine had to learn a new skill. "I had to sustain the conflict — not agree until I was sure. I knew how to stay in conflict in business but not in my primary relationship. I was so patterned to respond to my ex's anger or discomfort that I had to work hard to respond differently."

Elaine feared that the mortgage on the family home would be too costly for her. She also found it hard to know what was fair in sharing the boys' costs. Fortunately, she discovered an online site called Our Family Wizard, which included a shared calendar and places to record expenses. Tracking what each spent got them away from the "I'm paying more" issue. Over time, they saw that they were paying about the same.

Elaine received nourishment from those around her. "I got a lot of support from friends — they cooked and shared their strategies and experiences. I remember hearing, 'Yes, I get that you're angry, but you're probably not going to get what you want if you say that.' My friends lifted and held me by hearing me vent, offering perspectives, and reiterating my value in the world. Spending time with those who had known me before as well as after my life with Greta made me feel safe. My friends saw me wounded and disabled, and stayed with me to help me become able again. Re-treasuring my friends has been a gift for me."

Since Elaine and Greta had not legally married, they didn't need a legal divorce. Having no prescribed process was freeing, but it also left a void. "I wish I had been better at setting boundaries earlier. I could have insisted on a process for how we divided up our belongings, for instance, much earlier than I did." After eighteen months they reached an agreement, but it was not legally binding.

There were positive things as well as struggles. They jointly celebrated holidays, like Christmas. Elaine and Greta took the boys to a wilderness lodge for their birthdays. Both mothers attended school meetings. Greta spent more time with the children than she had before.

The Big Job of Managing Feelings

In the first year, Elaine felt frustration and fear about how Greta's behaviour would impact the kids. "I knew she would need to do what she does with them and natural consequences would follow. At the same time, I wanted to keep the children from experiencing those natural consequences. Now I am somewhat more accepting. At least now she gets them to their soccer games. They have consistency in their lives." Elaine echoed other parents' stress in learning to let the other parent interact with the children in her own style.

Greta's emotional reactivity still bothered Elaine. "Disdain is a powerful dye that colours interactions, and I'm sure I don't always do a great job of keeping it to myself. But I consistently work to represent things so that the kids can make up their own minds, and I never, ever, actively disparage her. She does disparage me. So I am constantly trying to discern when to say something and when to let things slide. It's exhausting."

Elaine could trace progress over the two years, mentally and financially. She felt stable internally, even if not always externally. Sometimes it was a relief not having to organize her life to Greta's standards. "And I'm out of debt! My credit rating is my own again."

Tough Questions from the Children

Elaine's self-awareness helped her recognize what she was going through and talk effectively with her children. She helped them make sense of their experience, responding to questions and accusations about the ending of the marriage. "My children have gone after me for splitting up, for breaking my vows, and it was so not my idea! Stefan told me, 'If you're going to split up, then you shouldn't have kids — they aren't gonna like it, it won't work.' I had my own waves of feeling hurt and scared and that the whole separation wasn't fair. Trying to be emotionally there for the kids in their pain was so hard."

The boys' feelings had erupted in public, putting her on the spot when she and the boys went to Hawaii and attended a wedding. During the dinner, Stefan asked her what a wedding was. She said, "It's a series of promises that people make to each other to build a life on."

"*Oh!*" said Gavin loudly from several tables away. "Well, you didn't honour your promises, did you, Mom?! You broke your promises!"

She told him, "It's a different kind of promise. It's between two people, and it only works if both people hold it."

Afterward they talked, and Gavin burst into tears, letting out his fear that Greta would marry her new girlfriend and leave.

Elaine's steadiness anchored her sons. It allowed them to show her their deepest feelings. They didn't ask Greta about the split because, as Gavin said, "She's not so good at this kind of conversation." Elaine was the fulcrum, the point that they could rail against.

Elaine's Journey

Elaine learned to see time differently. She had never had a break from her sons before and had not wanted one. Time to herself was excruciating at first because it meant the loss of her children. Working with her therapist helped her see those periods as an opportunity. "Even if I sat on the couch and cried because the kids weren't there, it was a choice. I did that for a while. I started to ask, 'What are the things I would like to do that I haven't been able to do?' That was a big step. I take my dog for a walk, and it's a lovely way to start my day. I listen to music." As she accepted her new reality, Elaine found different choices to build into her life.

She grew in other areas, too. "Emotionally, I now know I have needs. I had just been living to take care of business, the kids, my partner. This was what I had wanted — I liked to feel I was doing good things in the world. That's different than someone asking, 'What do *you* want?' Now I have learned to set boundaries around what I am doing, and for whom."

Now there are good times. She feels strong. "I've let go of the righteous indignation and victim status; it's not where I wanted to live. I have been able to find another adult relationship that I enjoy. I felt saved before by the expansive life force in friendship. Now I am able to give back, and I feel joyous to do so."

Initially overwhelmed, Elaine deepened her self-management skills. She learned how to pay attention to her own needs, to stay in conflict with Greta, and to sort out what she should try to influence and what she should leave alone. She developed a way to respond to her boys' hard questions with tactful honesty in a way that respected their bonds to Greta. A huge journey.

WANDA'S STORY:
LESBIAN AND HETEROSEXUAL PARENTING, MIXED

decision-making • being "second mother"
empathy with dads

Thirty-eight-year-old Wanda said, "This has been a whole adventure in living my values."

Her story began ten years before her interview with me, when Wanda and her partner, Jasmine, joined their lives in a commitment ceremony that was deeply meaningful yet not recognized by law. Five years later, Jasmine became pregnant by a sperm donor and had a daughter, Zoe. Wanda adopted Zoe when the baby was six weeks old, to legally become Zoe's mother. They were a family.

Things got thorny eighteen months later when Jasmine left Wanda and married a man. Suddenly, Jasmine and Wanda had completely different expectations of how they would parent. Jasmine and her new husband wanted Wanda to give up her parental rights so that Zoe could be part of a "normal biological family." Their request wrung Wanda's heart. She wanted to keep on being a mother and have her daughter with her half-time.

The three adults sought competent supports to find a resolution. "We started by seeing a counsellor, who turned out to know nothing about same-sex adoption and looked at me as if I was crazy. We got out of there pretty quickly!" They then tried mediation, but it became a difficult negotiation and then a full legal process, including psychological evaluations. "I really wanted fifty-fifty, and Jasmine was okay with that as long as it was best for Zoe. We tried to arrive at a shared understanding of what 'best for Zoe' meant. That's tricky when the science doesn't agree on its meaning, and the counselling doesn't agree, and there is some manipulation going on. The fifty-fifty started to unravel, and I realized I needed a lawyer."

Wanda's lawyer told her that the courts, in trying to reduce conflict, don't readily support fifty-fifty unless both parents want it. Rather than keep fighting for equal time, Wanda agreed to a one-third/two-thirds split of time. Zoe was almost five before the court processes finished.

Wanda's Determined Journey

Wanda wondered all along if this fight was worthwhile, if she should walk away and become some sort of aunt. She used counselling to sort out her feelings, and to confirm that she was bonded with Zoe and absolutely wanted to be in her life as her parent.

Counselling also allowed Wanda to find her feelings of shame that she and Jasmine hadn't made the marriage work, with an added pressure because they had been a lesbian couple. She had shame, too, that she wasn't the biological mother. "I kept getting the message, 'Open your heart and let go so that your daughter can have a normal family.' It was as if Jasmine and her husband thought that if they told this story enough, this other person (who was kind of a mistake) would disappear. I needed to assert my role as a mom to Zoe."

Fortunately, Wanda received lots of support. Her circle of mainly heterosexual, intact families reminded her what she knew intellectually — that there are many ways to be a family. "It helped that people cared, that they treated me the same as everyone else. They supported and loved me, assuring me that I was a great mom, and helped us buy a home. They would tell Zoe, 'We were at Mom and Momma's wedding.'"

Friends helped in practical ways, bringing Wanda a birthday gift from Zoe when she was too young to buy it herself. They did things that the other parent would do in an intact family, and it made a big difference to Wanda. Zoe's school recognized her family's unique structure by having a binder ready for each mother at the school orientation.

She also had to figure out what it meant to be Zoe's second mother. "Not being the 'alpha' or 'real' mother was hard. Normally I went with Zoe to her toddler class, but one week I couldn't go, so Jasmine took her. Another mother asked her, 'Are you her real mother? You look like her.... Is Wanda the nanny?' and Jasmine said, 'Yes,' and let it go." Biology had more power than adoption, no matter how loving.

Worried that Zoe might feel shame about having two mothers, Wanda told Zoe about her birth in a way that had no shame attached. "Every night for a period of time when she was two and three, I told her the kid version of her conception and birth: who came to her birthday parties, what friends brought. It was her bedtime story and she asked for it often. In fifth grade when each child gave a presentation about their family background, Zoe told her story: 'When I was born I had two moms, and when I was eighteen months old, they divorced.' I could hear that she understood the story and it was matter-of-fact."

Because she had Zoe less than 50 percent of the time, Wanda paid child support. She resented having to pay, since she wanted equal time. She found it hard to talk about money, even things like saving for college, with her co-parents because she didn't trust them. She felt they had played the rules to hurt her financially.

Wanda's Personal Growth

Wanda's unusual status in the divorce complicated her grieving. "There was so much sadness at first. I would go into Zoe's little room when she wasn't there and feel so lonely."

Wanda learned through counselling that it mattered that she was healthy and that taking care of herself was best for Zoe. She spent time with friends, letting them nurture her. She realized she had incredible resilience. "With support and a night's sleep, I kept getting back up. At some point I had to stop playing the victim — take my space and own my mistakes, my desires, and my powers."

Majority time with kids trumped minority time, and she experienced new empathy with dads. As the part-time parent, she felt she could never catch up. "When you only show up at the playground once a week, nobody knows who you are, even if they recognize your kid. I felt shame at not being the primary parent, especially where there were lots of stay-at-home moms."

Even with its drawbacks, sharing parenting paid off. Wanda was able to rest, sleeping in every Saturday. She was able to travel for her work. On days when Wanda had Zoe, she could focus on her, building a strong bond in a one-on-one relationship. Zoe felt loved and secure in both of her families.

Wanda's growth included social and legal awareness, as well as improved self-management skills. She took responsibility for her mistakes and worked through her feelings of shame. Wanda's self-awareness helped her make the challenging and painful decisions needed to craft her role of second mother. Her courage and willingness to seek support helped her to create the best world for Zoe and herself.

What Do These Stories Tell Us?

Almost all mothers feel the weight of society's — and their own — expectations to be stellar. Lesbian mothers Marian, Elaine, and Wanda felt an extra need to be exemplary as role models and visible pioneers. Also, in order to become pregnant, they had sought out invasive physical procedures. Each felt an intense need to make their family work. It was, therefore, extraordinarily painful to acknowledge the breakdown of the relationship. It took extra courage to accept the new reality.

Marian and her partner shared similar expectations of co-parenting and fairly high self-management skills. They kept the focus on their daughter and avoided open conflict. Marian's biggest challenge was to grieve the loss of their intact family and rebuild a new life. She found that meeting her daughter's needs kept her in the present and helped her survive.

Elaine had more losses to navigate, as business, parenting, and home had all been shared with Greta. Like Marian, Elaine found that her children's needs anchored her in the early days of overwhelming feelings. By reaching out in many directions, Elaine found support and learned new self-management skills. Her parenting abilities were tested by tough questions from her children about the separation, and she worked hard to give them meaningful answers that didn't hurt their relationship with Greta.

Wanda blazed a new trail in being an adoptive mother who wasn't the only mother when the family split up. "It's tricky for lesbians who become moms. You've been socialized to be the primary parent — not to be the dad. And when there's no room for two primary parents, it's tough. I'm supposed to be a mom, but there isn't room for me to be one. Our social roles come up every day." Being a non-primary mother wasn't something Wanda could figure out and settle into. She needed to adapt in every new social situation and keep creating her role.

All three mothers felt deep satisfaction with their growth and their children's well-being. Given the extra pressures on each, I was impressed at their ability to survive, develop, and co-parent.

10 Co-Operation, Survival, and Growth

The family is pieces of a puzzle that aren't connected.
Think of the whole.

— CARTER

If you have been in a long-term relationship, you know that when you and your partner are out of harmony with each other, every decision — such as who gets to park in the driveway — can be a source of lively dispute.

Ending a marriage raises scores of questions. The required decisions may feel as big and unwelcome as a dark mass on a chest X-ray. You know you have to choose your next steps, but none look good. Who will move? How far apart will the new homes be? What will the children's schedule look like? Even parents who are trying to avoid conflicts and focus on creating new lives can find themselves triggered during discussions.

In the following stories, the fathers and mothers showed many self-management skills. Ayla and Andrew were able to fully separate their conflicts from their parenting, which gave them many choices. Veronica approached divorce determined to avoid conflict completely. She believed that the compromises she made paid off for her children. Carter, with support from others, got through his grief so he could share parenting with Georgia, minimizing the emotional impacts of the divorce on their daughter. These parents' ability to keep their differences from impinging on their child-rearing helped their children thrive. Jonathon and Terry both put the interests of their son, Alden, first as much as possible. Terry's remarriage and her recurring depression added challenges, as did their shared preference for keeping feelings private.

It still wasn't easy. Issues such as money or scheduling wove through discussions, surfacing intensely for a while, and then subsiding.

AYLA'S STORY: EASIER THAN MANY

shared expectations
introducing new partners successfully

For Ayla and Andrew, divorcing was difficult but co-parenting was not. Their girls were six and two years old at the separation. The parents felt that the children needed them both, and were clear that they didn't want their kids to have a main and a secondary base, but two homes. "We were committed that they wouldn't take luggage back and forth between us so they wouldn't feel like they were visiting," Ayla said. "We were completely in tune about parenting all along … but not about other things," she added dryly.

The parents' shared expectations and trust on parenting issues made possible some unusual choices. Early on, their older daughter said that the hardest part for her was eating with only one or the other parent. So Ayla and Andrew started having dinner together once a month.

They responded jointly to other requests. "My older girl was distressed that we weren't together and asked us to hug. We did, to reassure her that we don't hate each other. Then she said, 'Will you kiss each other?' which we didn't do! We had to set some boundaries. She was upset at feeling that so many things were out of her control."

Now, six years later, both parents are remarried and take some shared vacations that include the parents, new spouses, and children. Ayla knew this wasn't something every divorced parent could do, but she was happy that it worked for her family. She and Andrew deliberately redefined *family* to mean "a group of people who care about each other."

Ayla said, "It didn't feel like a negotiation, we didn't disagree on much to do with parenting. We made a commitment that we would put them first. Any arguments we took out of their earshot. It took a lot of maturity; we needed not to be insecure. We both wanted to minimize the damage to the kids."

Managing Impacts on the Children

The girls saw both parents often. "We get along, and they see us laughing, that we are still friends. I am close to them, and they have an awesome relationship with their dad." Such relaxed warmth was only possible because of both parents' high self-management skills, which limited open strife.

The parents developed a deliberate strategy for introducing new partners to the children. They agreed that neither would have the children meet any new romantic partner until the relationship was serious. At that point, the new partner would meet the other parent (the ex) before the kids did. "We gave them permission to develop a relationship with the new person with no worries."

The new stepmom of Ayla's kids, Bettina, told Ayla that she didn't think she would have been accepted so well if Ayla had been neutral in referring to her. Instead, Ayla told her girls, "I've met Bettina, I think she's really nice."

Ayla's Journey

Early days post-split were hard for Ayla as she grieved the loss of family, and she found herself leaning on her kids. "My children were my safety net when I was flailing around. I felt bad about that; I know that comes with consequences to the kids. Beyond that, the divorce was just hard. Knowing that I had shaken the foundation of the children's lives, that I was the source of the hurt, was hard. Co-parenting was second-best."

Extra losses meant Ayla needed extra support. "My mother, father, and grandfather all died within one year of our divorce, so I struggled to absorb that grief. Friends helped by coming around to take the kids, which took the pressure off me. They also were encouraging and complimentary about how we were handling the co-parenting. They saw the kids being happy; this validation meant a lot."

Ayla was clear about her goals. "I wanted to be divorced and I wanted to be a mother. I've never felt the ache of being away from the kids as some people do. Perhaps the nature of our co-parenting helps. There is no anxiety."

Ayla believed that co-parenting allowed her to be a better mother. "There is time when I can do whatever I want. I need a break after time with the kids, to take care of myself. The more self I have that is healthy, the more I have to give to my children."

Two factors helped this family. The parents held similar expectations about how co-parenting should work, and they both already had high self-management skills. This let them keep their disagreements about their relationship separate from their parenting. That's a big deal. Their children benefited from seeing them together, relaxed and enjoying the other's company.

Their strategy for introducing new partners seemed generous in spirit, and helped their children adapt to their changing families. Ayla had other challenges the first year from family losses, which added to her grief from the divorce. It wasn't easy, but certainly less painful than many stories here.

VERONICA'S STORY: AVOIDING CONFLICT AT ALL COSTS

decision-making • lots of contact • no fighting

Veronica and Stanley separated when their sons were nine and eleven. At our interview twenty years later, Veronica told me she had watched her sister's bitter divorce and been horrified at the impact on her niece and nephew. Veronica, a self-possessed teacher, worked with adolescents and had seen the results there, too, of poor adult decisions. While some other parents made choices to minimize conflict, Veronica's determination to avoid arguments was particularly strong. It shaped the parenting that followed. She would have given her children up entirely, if necessary, to avoid a custody battle. "As long as there's no fighting. I wouldn't put them in the middle of a court battle."

When the couple separated, Stanley moved into a nearby apartment while Veronica stayed in the family home. Veronica and Stanley shared similar values and expectations about the children's care, so decisions went fairly smoothly on how they would co-parent. The boys would spend two to three days at each home, then shift.

They planned the transition from one home to two jointly and carefully. They prepared the new apartment before telling their children of the split, as advised by their counsellor. Then all four went to view the new place. The boys got to discuss which furniture would stay in their rooms in the original home and which would go to the apartment. Veronica thought they accepted the separation pretty well.

For her it was harder. "At first it was a lot of work to be civil to Stanley — it was far easier to be angry. I kept telling myself, 'This isn't about what's right, it's about making it easier for the kids. If they are accepting it, I can too.'" She worried about them being hurt or damaged, but believed that it's how a situation is handled, not what's happened, that determines outcomes.

After a year, Stanley showed up at Veronica's house one Friday afternoon. He began, "My work schedule is shifting to weekend work and it looks permanent. I want to change our arrangement. The kids will need to spend three-day weekends with you, the rest of the weekdays with me." Veronica's heart sank.

"But … they've settle in so well! This is working great."

"They have, but they'll adjust. We've made one way work; we can make another way work."

Veronica was aghast. She couldn't imagine all those weeknights without the boys, without her asking about homework and lunches. Her stomach churning, she reminded herself, "As long as there are no fights." She nodded stiffly and swallowed her distress.

The boys shifted to the new schedule, which remained in place until they were grown. Overall it worked, but for Veronica there was a price. "I missed the children a lot during the week." She used her evenings to cook and read, but the ache didn't fade for many years.

Veronica and Stanley sustained their joint involvement in the boys' lives and spent regular time as a foursome. They held frequent family dinners, and attended school events and parent-teacher meetings together.

Impacts on the Children

Like many parents, Veronica was curious about how her sons truly felt about what had happened. One year post-split, twelve-year-old Gord was assigned a paper for school. He chose to write on his parents' separation. Veronica wondered nervously what he would write. He went to his grandmother for help, and his teacher liked the resulting essay so much that she requested a copy. In his paper, Gord talked about the benefits of the separation: two homes, with two different video game systems; each parent doing things with him; and having the full attention of each parent when they were together. The costs? He wrote, "I miss them being together … but there is no fighting." Veronica softened with relief as she read it.

A year later, she and the boys were sitting on the couch watching a movie about two kids trying to get their parents back together. She asked casually, "Did you want us to get back together?"

"You guys are always getting together!" they answered. "Would we get to keep our duplicate stuff?"

She concluded wryly that no huge emotional problems were lurking below the surface. She also saw that the minor acting-out that Gord had displayed before the separation had disappeared. He seemed more co-operative around the house, too. Even with this reassuring evidence, she carried the question, "Was this the right thing to do?" for many years.

Her Later Verdict

Over time, Veronica relaxed. She saw the boys doing well, and learned that she could survive on her own. She began to appreciate her increased freedom, and made a month-long dream trip to New Zealand without guilt, knowing her sons were in good hands with their father. As the boys matured, they finished university studies and seemed well-adjusted.

Veronica felt good about the early decisions she had made to avoid conflict. "The two homes gave the kids their best version of family."

Veronica and Stanley's shared expectation that they would keep having family events together created a reassuring base for their sons. Both parents had the self-management skills to shift smoothly from living in one home to two. Veronica's absolute determination to avoid conflict, based on her sister's experience, produced co-parenting that seems to have succeeded. There may have been other solutions if the parents had been willing to enter mediation and look for them. As it was, Veronica paid a price in loneliness to achieve her goal of protecting her sons from conflict. It wasn't perfect, but this family found a way through that worked for them.

CARTER'S STORY:
CARVING A NEW PATH

evolving schedules • help from family
growing co-operation

Carter, a fit and ambitious thirty-six-year-old parole officer, had separated from his wife, Georgia, ten years before our interview. With help, he survived his grief about the divorce and gained a broader perspective, which guided his actions.

Their daughter, Sandra, was a year old when her parents split up. Both parents wanted to avoid the courts and put Sandra first. Although Carter wanted to have equal time with his daughter, he knew Georgia was still nursing her. He believed it would benefit Sandra for the nursing to continue for a while, so he postponed discussions of more equal time until the breastfeeding ended.

Carter's Journey

The pain of separation tested Carter. Co-parenting meant he saw his ex often. "Figuring out how to accept that the marriage wasn't working, and grieving that — and still being there for my daughter — was hard. During the early months, I had to see Georgia; I couldn't escape the contact with her. I even thought of taking a job in Toronto to get away from that pain."

His father's advice made him consider his decisions carefully: "Don't badmouth your ex or her family; be respectful; be supportive."

Carter chose to stay in Vancouver.

He found support, particularly in the first six months, in talking with his father and other older adults. He had thought that the marriage might be fixable, but that hope faded. He visited regularly with his parents to keep himself going. They reassured him that the grief and fear he was feeling would ease. "It felt like I was carving a path in a jungle, without knowing what was coming next. There was lots of uncertainty and fear: is there a cliff there? I wasn't sure if any little thing would mess things up or turn into a legal battle." A co-worker told him, "Write down all the good and bad. Get it out of your system, then burn it." His friends also helped by supporting him and being respectful of Georgia — they didn't trash-talk her.

Even in his pain, Carter knew that what he and Georgia did as parents was distinct from their marital relationship. "At the beginning, I had lots of self-doubt. I was trying to make sure we were separating the *parenting* from the *conflict*. During conflicts, my goal was that what Sandra saw between her parents would not disturb her — that she would never feel that she had to pick sides between us. Even for things like flu shots, Georgia and I checked with each other: is this in her interest? We try not to make it a power struggle, not be selfish."

Despite all the parents' efforts, the split impacted their daughter. "It was so hard for Sandra; she couldn't understand why her parents weren't together. She would try to make us hold hands. [Poignant pause.] We both told each other when she said things to us about our relationship so we'd know what was going on for her."

Evolving Arrangements

At first the parents disagreed about finances. "For about three years, I was paying a larger share, more than I felt was fair, because I was earning more. Georgia went on the internet and showed me charts of what the court would say. I believed her and went with it, though I wasn't happy."

Parenting time and finances kept evolving. For the first year, Sandra was with Georgia on weekdays and with Carter on weekends. When Sandra turned two, they adopted a Sunday-to-Wednesday/Thursday-to-Saturday schedule. Once parenting time equalized, finances became fairly straightforward. Carter and Georgia switched levels of contribution according to who was earning more. They also both tried to be flexible around work schedules, including shifts, so that neither of them would need to use child care much. Carter said, "I don't get a sitter when I'm with Sandra, I see all of her I can. I don't regret that."

After three years, Georgia brought a fiancé onto the scene. Carter, while not happy about this development, treated him well. This was partly because he knew and respected the fiancé and partly because he had become more trusting of Georgia. "She was there for me; she sacrificed for me and my schooling. We still support each other, and over time the trust has increased." Being courteous in acknowledging her new partner was a significant way for Carter to support Georgia.

Win-Win Help from Grandma

Transitions happened at Grandma's house (Georgia's mother), to everyone's benefit. One parent would drop Sandra off at Grandma's house. The grandmother took her to school and picked her up, with the other parent picking Sandra up after work, if it was a changeover day. This meant that the parents could live some distance from each other and still keep a feasible schedule for Sandra. It also meant that Sandra's grandmother could be part of her granddaughter's life.

Impacts on Father and Daughter

Carter felt grateful and positive about the outcomes for Sandra and himself. "I get to share in all aspects of her life. I am a dad and full partner in her parenting. Sandra gets to have a dad who is a big part of her life. She is better off for that." His only regret was not having moved closer to Georgia's house, as he felt he may have missed some things from living farther away.

Carter had increased his ability to take others' needs into account. "I have become a more compassionate and understanding person. I have more respect for what it means to have a family, to be a dad. I can't imagine not having her there now: school, soccer, and huge, affectionate hugs. If you're having a rough day, a hug from your daughter puts it all in perspective."

His advice for others facing this challenge: "Be patient. It takes work. Be selfless. Adapt as challenges and opportunities come up and expect wrinkles. There is no perfect solution, and it changes all the time. Help the other parent — you're doing it for the family. The family is pieces of a puzzle that aren't connected. Think of the whole."

Carter and Georgia's shared expectation to co-parent made things easier for everyone. Carter initially struggled with his grief and anger. Support and suggestions from family, friends, and co-workers increased his ability to accept reality and to take into account the needs of others — both crucial self-management skills. He developed a perspective that included both Sandra and Georgia. That broader view helped him make decisions, such as not moving away, and reminded him always to speak respectfully of Georgia. Such decisions meant Sandra kept a good relationship with both of her parents and had ample time with each. Carter gained deep satisfaction from his father role, and joy in his bond with Sandra.

JONATHON AND TERRY'S STORIES: TWO PERSPECTIVES ON QUIET SHARING

focus on children • depression • finances

Jonathon and Terry separated twenty years before each of them told me their stories. Their son, Alden, was now twenty-five. Both seemed introverted and private, with enough self-management skills to be thoughtful of their impacts on Alden as he grew up. Terry's intermittent depression decreased her ability to mother in the way she wanted to.

The parents' communication and relationship problems had intensified over several years until Terry finally moved out of the family home, taking five-year-old Alden with her. At that point, Jonathon felt that Alden was bonded more closely with his mother than with him. "I thought it would be natural for him to live with his mother." He was content as long as Alden could spend time with him whenever he wanted, which Terry supported and made possible.

The parents' negotiations showed their ability to put their son's needs first. "His mom and I felt that our separation should have the smallest possible impact on him. We had decided not to deny him anything other than our presence as a family." Their shared expectations simplified the planning.

When the three began living the new agreement, Jonathon had jumbled feelings. "What Alden wanted was to have his family. I felt both happy that I could continue to be with Alden when he so desired, and sad and bitter because the family life was not working out for either parent." He worried about Alden. "It was awkward because whatever was going on, it was not my son's fault, and I did not want him to take on any sense of responsibility."

Jonathon struggled to find a meaningful role when he was not with Alden. "I felt bewildered, as I had so little to do that seemed of value when my son was not with me." After two years, Alden began living weekdays with his mother and weekends with his father, and Jonathon felt satisfied that he was caregiving the best he could. All three also spent time together. "When we were all together, I felt I had nothing to say. It felt like it didn't matter, and I did not like being silent."

Three years passed, and Terry remarried and had a baby girl. Alden moved to live mainly with his dad. For several years, Terry, her new husband, and her daughter lived across the street from Jonathon so that Alden could easily go back and forth between the houses. Terry remembered this as a good time for the family. "Alden's dad often had my daughter at his house and took lots of photos of both children. One picture in particular showed both children at a picnic table outside his house. The picture reminds me that Alden's dad and I remained friends, that the children had good times with him and with each other. The children were loved and felt loved. They had a lot of freedom and met other children in the street. I am glad that in spite of all the drama, they could be completely in the moment, relaxed, happy, and playful. It's wonderful that there was support and trust, that they were safe and happy, even if their parents were separated."

Money was sparse for Terry. "I was struggling for many years as a stay-at-home mother. I went back to school as soon as my daughter started kindergarten. I always felt poor; it still seems somewhat unfair."

Jonathon saw things differently. "Sometimes I felt that Alden was left aside when his younger sister was present. He had been an only child with two parents looking after his needs, and then there was only one parent when he was with me and only a half when he was with his mother. Terry and I both believed that Penelope Leach was right when she encouraged parents to give to their children when young so that later they will be more independent. She and I talked about Leach's needs theory, but there was not much else we could do about her having two children."

Finances didn't bother him. "I always felt that if I took care of myself, then there would be enough to help Alden, and Alden with his mom, on whatever basis was needed. Money was not something that we squabbled about. If we didn't have it, then we just didn't at that particular time."

Terry's second marriage ended and she soon moved to a lakefront cottage with both children. She had suffered from depression for a number of years during and after her marriages, which now deepened. "I had a strong desire to be quiet and turn to the wisdom within. I just stared at the lake. The metaphor of 'licking my wounds' came to mind a lot." Terry expressed wistful dissatisfaction with her own parenting: "I wish I had been less depressed and more outgoing. The two children often played by themselves, while I stared at the lake."

As Terry had two children to nurture and little energy available to cope, conflict between mother and son began to intensify. When Alden turned twelve, he decided to move in with his father. Terry felt hurt, but tried to keep Alden's needs in mind. "It was very painful that Alden left, but I was reading Robert Bly's *Iron John: A Book about Men* and realized how important it was for him to be with his father." Alden began attending an experimental school that provided a consistent community of support for him through his teen years.

Terry began finding ways to heal and grow. "I remembered the bag of clay I had bought some time before, and I started coiling big pots. These pots helped me contain my feelings and pain. During this time, I had a strong feeling that I was doing healing work, my own therapy. I journaled almost daily about my pain, depression, thoughts, insights into my artwork, and I devoured self-help books. All of these contributed to my well-being."

Terry returned to school after two years. "I enrolled in a master's program for art therapy. The program consisted of discussions, writing, research, and I also kept my own artwork and self-healing going. I realized then that I am born to be a single mother, more a mother than a lover or wife, more an individual than part of a couple."

Jonathon's life also began evolving: he started dating. "Doing that meant I was definitely having a different lifestyle. This fulfilled my sense of exploring the world." His best times were having fun with Alden, and his new life as a single dad.

Success and Some Misgivings

Both parents sounded subdued when they looked back. Their voices held relief and satisfaction that Alden had grown into a thoughtful, responsible young man. There was also regret that there may have been better paths, but they hadn't found them.

This couple's style of interaction was to leave much unsaid, and Terry felt sorry that they had not sought outside help. "Find a really good counsellor who is skilled at getting both partners to open up and communicate from the heart. Much of what happened had to do with not being heard, not being talked to."

Terry's personal growth helped but didn't banish her depression. Fighting depression was, for her, the hardest aspect of co-parenting. She grieved that Alden was affected by it.

Jonathon knew that the separation had hurt Alden. He also saw benefits of his co-operation with Terry. "I know that Alden always appreciated that we remained friends." Jonathon and Terry both felt they had done their best with Alden, and each had regrets. Both parents had enough self-management skills to set aside their own wishes for time with Alden when they thought Alden would be better off with the other parent. When Terry's depression intensified for a few years, Alden moved back with his father. This was a good option for him, but it added another relocation to a string of frequent moves that ended only when Alden entered his teens.

Both parents relied on books and their own inner resources for support and growth, not comfortable with bringing in other people to assist them in this way. I sensed some wistfulness that they had not sought, and found, more answers. Bringing in outsiders can never guarantee success, but, as in the case of Janice in Chapter 5, when you are experiencing something that many others have encountered, taking the risk of seeking help may provide new, better answers. Yet Jonathon and Terry took comfort that they were able to keep Alden's interests in focus, and maintain enough of a bond between them to nurture Alden to maturity.

What Do These Stories Tell Us?

This chapter is titled "Co-Operation, Survival, and Growth." All four sets of parents struggled and found a way forward that allowed their children to be close to them both, co-operating in many ways.

They all dealt with unique factors in their lives. The death of Ayla's father, mother, and grandfather after she and her husband separated amplified her feelings of loss. She acknowledged that she leaned on her children for a while, and then recovered to co-parent amiably with her ex. Veronica's prior exposure to her sister's divorced parenting strongly influenced her decisions and led her to avoid conflict at all costs. In Carter's situation, his openness to advice from older adults influenced him to remain living nearby and adopt a view of the whole family, which allowed him to co-parent closely with Georgia. Terry's struggle with depression added extra challenges for her and Jonathon. They both had regrets but nevertheless managed to provide Alden with enough love and consistency for him to grow into a successful adult.

Each parent kept the focus on the children, containing conflicts so they didn't dominate the family. They co-operated with the other parent, sustaining a tone of respect, using and expanding their self-management skills as they were able. There were no villains here, just mothers and fathers feeling relieved satisfaction at their children's development.

11 The Silver Lining: Growing as Parents

I am not what happened to me; I am what I choose to become.
— UNKNOWN

We can teach our children only what we have already learned ourselves. This is a central truth of being a parent. Our children soak in who we are and how we are. Do we worry about the feelings of others, or stride ahead regardless, intent on our goals? Do we stay focused every minute of the day, or stop for a deep breath of morning air? Do we sacrifice our beliefs to gain acceptance, or stand firm? Our children absorb these lessons, and many more, from being in our presence.

Why is this important for co-parenting? Because these stories show that as they walked the co-parent path, many mothers and fathers learned new things about themselves and found different ways to respond to their world. They stepped into increased confidence, self-management, and even joy. These hard-won rewards were gifts they could model and transmit to their children. More than a silver lining, the growth became the richest possible nourishment for their lives.

Personal growth? Oh, yes.

The stories in every chapter contain growth. Those below, while differing in many respects, are particularly full of new understandings and enhanced skills.

ANGELA'S STORY:
FROM FULL-TIME MOTHER TO NEW CONFIDENCE

exploration • financial fears • growth

Angela, at fifty-five, was lean, with fine features. The tension in her voice throughout our interview reflected her determination to be a good mother and create a financially stable life for herself. At that time, she was five years post-divorce. Her son was sixteen and her daughter, twenty.

During Angela's marriage with Franklin, his banking work required significant travel, long hours, and geographic moves every few years. Angela mused, "I had to adapt — it was the hallmark of my marriage. The frequent moves really undermined me. I felt more and more dependent on him after each move as my supports became sparser and more distant." She believed that someone needed to manage all the needs arising from the many moves, such as finding a pediatrician and getting the children started in new schools. She quit her job when her daughter was four. "I lay awake many nights, feeling I was cutting a safety net. In choosing the life of a full-time mom, I became financially dependent on my husband and reduced my own ability to make a living. Yet under the same circumstances, I would make exactly that choice again."

Franklin ended the twenty-year marriage by moving out. After eighteen months of negotiation, the parents signed divorce papers in 2005. As Angela had been the primary parent, they agreed the children would spend every second weekend with their dad, and half of vacation times. The remaining time they would be with Angela. "We had no issues about the parenting; the conflict was all about money." Angela remembered weeks of intense negotiations, where she worked seven days a week to understand the exact issues involved. Her role in household finances had withered over the years. "I started out paying all the bills, and then by the end I wasn't."

The separation devastated Angela. She found counselling for herself and for her children. "I relied on the therapist week to week. Sometimes, when I couldn't make it through a day, I would call him in tears. I was terrified about what would happen. I was fifty years old. Financial fears were the greatest, and still haven't really gone away."

One friend helped her weather the early months. "I had a sweetheart of a friend who lived two doors down. The summer my husband moved out, she stopped by every few days. She would knock at the door and call, 'Just checking in.' It meant so much to me. It moved our friendship to a deeper level."

Angela vigorously avoided blaming Franklin in conversations with her children, determined not to show Franklin in any worse light than she showed herself. "I wish that we'd had more skilled therapists before the divorce, so we would have been better at just recognizing each other, and finding ways to honour each other."

Impacts on the Children

Krista, an expressive fifteen-year-old, let Angela know she was finding the divorce hard. Every time she came from her dad's, she would cry for two hours. Rolf, younger and more reserved, didn't show his feelings directly. Three years later, graduating from grade nine, he wrote, "My greatest accomplishment was getting through my parents' divorce."

Angela helped her kids deal with further changes. Four months after the divorce was final, Franklin told Angela and the kids that he was going to remarry. When Krista heard the news, she sank to the floor. "How many more things do we have to absorb? I'm supposed to be a bridesmaid. Everyone there will be celebrating; for Rolf and me, it will be like a funeral!"

Angela felt she had done well in recognizing what the kids were experiencing. "I told them, 'No matter how wacky this feels, it's your father. I want you to have the best relationship you can possibly have with him.'" She helped them pick out dressy clothes for the wedding, and plan what to say. Krista, with her mother's support, prepared to tell her father, "I need you to know I'm excited for you, and I'm not in the same place — there's only so much I can do." Krista told her mother afterward, "You're like my therapist."

Angela's Journey

Angela, already self-aware, found that parenting kept bringing her new insights. When her daughter was sixteen, Angela went back to work. Mother and daughter began to clash. "It was humbling," recalled Angela. "I was working in a non-profit to save the world. Krista was only into celebrities. My disdain for her came through; I wasn't willing to set aside my beliefs to enter her world. I realized the rift between us was getting bigger. One day I walked into her room and said, 'I have a cousin in Philadelphia who does fashion design. Would you like to go visit her?' It was my first reaching out into her world, setting aside my beliefs about who she should be and accepting her view of herself."

She credited counselling with much of her growth. "I have moved to another level. Before, I had a bout of depression, feeling unheard. Here, I learned to identify my needs and reach out to get them met, and not feel ashamed. I learned how to build networks. Now I feel more at peace and expansive. I have learned the tremendous power of saying 'I don't know' and 'I care about you.'"

This deepened ability to reach out helped her to support a friend struggling with breast cancer. They talked on the phone over a period of months. "She told me her deepest fears. We were two people at the bottom of the well, being very honest with each other. We would send poetry back and forth. We talked of how we felt vitally heard by the other."

Her self-awareness showed again in an incident with her daughter when Krista was seventeen. "Our relationship was really sound by then. I went with her to preview a possible university. I sat with her, listening to all this peace and idealism, thinking, *This is so not her!* Afterward I told her, 'Don't worry, I won't try to sell you on this one, I know this isn't your thing.' And she smiled and said, 'But it would have been yours, wouldn't it, Mom?' We had a real respect for each other's differences." Such a precious moment of connection.

Finances continued to worry Angela. She had received a lump-sum support payment with the divorce, but hadn't expected how hard it would be in her fifties to find a foothold in the workforce. Her new confidence and self-awareness hadn't yet translated into work that paid enough for her to relax about her future. Her financial fears didn't keep her from enjoying her life, though. She decided to take salsa lessons. "The joy from dancing was exquisite. You're moving to music and it's wonderful. I felt feminine, attractive, worth a million bucks."

Angela concluded, "Some of this wisdom comes with age, I guess. Earlier I would be about climbing the mountain, striving to achieve a goal; now I'll slide down the other side on my butt, and have a good time."

I admired how Angela kept growing. She made sure not to portray her ex as a bad guy to her kids and supported them skillfully. She kept increasing her self-management and emotional skills, accepting responsibility for her choices and finding ways to move toward her goals. She enjoyed a close relationship with her adult children. Though she hadn't resolved all of her questions, she had developed a deepened confidence in herself and her future.

LYN'S STORY:
DIFFICULT, BUT NOT DEVASTATING

slow transitions • flexibility
talking with the children

Lyn and Lincoln had decided to separate two years before Lyn's interview with me. A savvy forty-three-year-old, Lyn had been a stay-at-home mother until their sons were twelve and thirteen, when she and Lincoln separated. The parents took their time and found that a slow transition to co-parenting worked well.

Lyn had known the marriage was ending for many years. "I struggled a lot with guilt before leaving. I asked myself what example I was setting for the boys by staying in a dysfunctional relationship (not violent, just not there). By leaving, I would model taking action on what is important … and hopefully finding a functional relationship down the road. In the long run, I knew this was not only better for me but for them, because they would see two happier people."

The couple's history impacted their choices. "Because of how Linc's previous divorce had worked — his daughter had gone much more with her mother than with him — I knew he would want at least 50 percent. It would have been a big fight if I had wanted them full-time, so I stayed in the marriage until I was willing to consider having the kids less than that. I saw what Linc went through in his contentious first divorce, and I wanted our divorce to be different."

The parents took a year to figure things out. "I know it doesn't work for everyone to stay in the same home, but it helped us because we could get used to things before diving in. Our decisions happened organically over time, instead of our having to talk about everything in one two-hour discussion. Our kids didn't know in the fall, but by spring they did. We went on our planned family vacation at Easter. In summer we started taking separate vacations. Finally my husband moved out; I left the house when the possession date came up one year ago."

In working together to make a schedule, the parents learned from Linc's experience with his daughter, now nineteen. "She was with him every second weekend and every Wednesday. The weekend worked okay, but the Wednesdays were a disaster. She wouldn't even begin to settle in before she left again." They chose week-on/week-off with holidays split.

The parents lived ten minutes apart by car, and did whatever they could to keep things easy. "Even during weeks when they are with Linc, I will get them from school and keep them till their dad picks them up. During their weeks with me, Linc sees them when he has extra time."

Lyn chose to fill in any gaps in the kids' schedule, regardless of the formal arrangement. This reduced her time available to build her business. "Before, I was not working. Now I am juggling being the mom, organizing the kids' schedules, managing doctor and dentist appointments, and working at a business driven by me. That's difficult. If I don't make something happen in the business, nothing happens."

Making It Work for the Kids

She believed the arrangement, though imperfect, was working. "It's important for kids to see both parents because they love us both. I had to put my feelings in the back seat and look at what would be best emotionally for the kids, knowing this wasn't their choice. We both wanted the kids to know that they are loved, that they aren't pawns, and to feel comfortable with each of us."

When Lyn asked the boys how it was going, they said they didn't like the transfer on Sundays, gathering their things and going to the other house. So, for the first year, Lyn did most of the packing and unpacking for them at her house. She knew they were old enough to do it themselves. "I wanted them to be fully unpacked in each house, the suitcase out of sight, so they wouldn't feel they were camping out for each week."

Lyn and Linc held keys to each other's houses. "Linc had trepidation about this initially, but it has worked out well. When the kids have forgotten something, which happens a lot, it takes so much anxiety out of the equation. It takes trust, though."

"Try it, and if it doesn't work, change it." This flexibility paid off for the first Christmas post-split. The boys were with Lyn on Christmas Day, and she planned to cook dinner, with Linc coming over to join them. "In the end we had dinner at his place, because it was bigger. I could see how great it was for the boys to see us together, and for us, too. It was comfortable enough."

Lyn saw costs and benefits for her sons. "I'm sure they miss the other parent during summer, during longer stays with each of us." She wasn't certain that they were noticing that both parents were happier. She felt more emotionally engaged with them than she had been before, when she was so full of her own concerns.

Lyn's Journey

Lyn also felt the price and the satisfactions for herself. "Initially I was not lonely, I was so happy to be out of the relationship. Now it sets in sometimes, especially when I don't have the kids in summer, wondering if I will ever be in another relationship. I have gained a lot of confidence, knowing that I will never again settle for less than what I want, that I honoured what was true for me. I've gained a ton of emotional freedom from hearing the voice that was always underneath and having the guts to act on it."

She learned a whole new skill: being a property owner. "I had never owned a place on my own, so I learned to arrange all you have to manage in owning a property. Last week my fridge water supply system failed, and we had a flood. Before, I would have called my husband, but now I had to figure it out myself. After a moment of panic, I realized I needed to handle it, and I did. I found an emotional strength I didn't know I had."

Lyn made careful decisions around property. It was important for her to own rather than rent. This choice brought whining from her kids their first summer post-split because she had less money available for recreation. "When we went to the beach, I'd say, 'Go off and play,' and they would be ready to go home after half an hour. They kept moaning, 'If we had a Jet Ski, if we were on a boat....'"

This made Lyn feel miserable and she feared what the remaining holiday would be like. But she tackled the complaining directly by taking responsibility for her decision: "I'm not saying this to make you feel bad, but I want you to know that I made a choice. I wanted to own a property here in Seattle, and so I can't provide these things for you right now. If you continue to say that, it will be hurtful to me."

The boys responded well to the new information, and Lyn relaxed. "Their dad has lots of great toys. It's so easy to see how parents start parenting from guilt."

Lyn let herself receive help from many people. "My support came from friends and coaching colleagues who asked me great questions about the choices I was making or what I wanted. They gave me lots of support in a detached way, so I felt free to make my decisions. And my mom — just knowing she was there.

"Our arrangement works for me because I have the kids a lot. It's great to have them, and then also good not to have them. At first I felt guilty relief that I could concentrate on things I needed to get done when they weren't there. Once I let the guilt go, I appreciated some opportunity to be on my own. I've had the chance to discover things about myself in those quiet times."

Lyn's experience changed her views on parenting after divorce. "Initially, I believed that co-parenting was going to be devastating. Now, living it, it's much better than I anticipated. It's been difficult, but not devastating. I've seen how much being flexible contributes to maintaining a reasonable relationship. I had witnessed rigidity in my husband's previous co-parenting and it didn't work. This is more doable."

She had gained trust in herself and her intuition, and found that she was stronger than she knew. "I've learned a lot of about what's important to me, what I am willing and not willing to negotiate on."

A high level of self-management skills in both parents allowed them to choose options that worked for everyone. Lyn put her own feelings aside, compromised to make things work, and explained her choices clearly to her sons. Linc's self-management skills made it possible for him to share the house with Lyn for a year and reach decisions slowly and thoughtfully. Together, they met their children's needs and their own.

IVAN'S STORY:
TENSIONS OVER TIME

power struggles • growth • legal system impact

Ivan, a fiftyish teacher with a rumpled appearance and an easy voice, described his separation ten years earlier. "Julia and I talked about splitting up nine or ten months before we did. I kept hoping things would resolve; I wondered if it was better to split or to hang in. There was no dramatic conflict, but love had been lost. I thought the kids would see that, consciously or unconsciously."

They stayed in the same house for the first year and a half. It had been a two-family house, so after separating they split the house again. "I was downstairs, Julia upstairs, and the kids had beds in both places. We chose that because it was easy for the girls. At eight and ten years old, they were pretty adaptable. There was no going back and forth between houses. We could keep dealing with household costs in a shared way."

He paused thoughtfully. "Sharing the house got us through the first eighteen months, but by then we wanted to escape the pain of not getting along and gain more emotional independence from each other. Neither of us was keen to move, but I did, finally, because most of the investment in the house was from her family. I temporarily rented the upstairs of a nearby house."

Who's Right?

The parents achieved major decisions on living space and finances fairly easily, yet tension persisted between them about the time split with the girls. "Negotiations focused on the time proportions — she wouldn't do fifty-fifty. Julia said that the kids needed her more than they needed me. She had the leverage of Massachusetts law, and according to my advisers (we were in mediation; we each had both counsellor and lawyer), if we went to court, the judge would favour the mother. So we did the best we could in mediation and stayed out of the courts."

Ivan ended up with 40 percent of the time with the girls, Julia 60 percent. Ivan felt trampled and dug in his heels. "I thought she was coming out ahead of me. I had never encountered this depth of gut-level fury that this person was trying to take my kids from me. I got so caught up in anger at her, I was determined not to give an inch. I was going by the letter of the law, not in the best interests of the girls. I haven't fully let go of that. I've always had suppressed anger at being pushed over by her and by the system — being discriminated against. It wasn't just her; it's the system which always leans toward the mother."

Because Ivan had some emotional distance from those years by the time we met, I asked him how much difference Julia's extra 10 percent of time had made, in the long term. He admitted, "It probably didn't matter one way or the other, for the kids' well-being." His voice held regret for the costs of ongoing tension and anger.

Ivan remembered his sadness. "There was incredible pain from being away from the girls, especially on holidays or summer vacations. It was hard to watch Julia with them. I dealt with the pain by burying myself in work."

He wanted to do everything right as a father, and now saw the cost of this, too. "For years I didn't fully live my life. I was so caught up in maintaining my power. There was an underlying tightness of needing to be the perfect dad. I tried to be there for the girls, and to show them the ugly side of me as little as possible. I question whether this was a good goal — if I had it to do over, I would shift it a bit. If I had been able to let go and know I didn't have to prove anything, I don't know how things would have been different."

Finding Ways to Grow and Let Go

Time helped Ivan. Teachers and friends did, too.

He learned to look at how he was shaping his life. "At first I was caught in my egocentric state in the negotiations on schedules: You can't do this to me. Gradually, as I could see those two young women growing up and making their own choices, I could let go and trust them more. I started to remake my life so that I wouldn't need them as much. Gradually, I got more healthy."

Ivan worked with a spiritual teacher for about a year. He went into professional development courses that also created powerful personal learning. He counted on a few old friends as well, for long-term support.

His learning paid off. "I had generally stuffed anger away. I have become better at being with strong emotions like anger; they don't hang around as long. When I started a yoga and meditation program to handle a new relationship, I learned that you can't do it all from your head. I shifted gears to learn more about the rest of me."

Now, with both daughters in university, Ivan was approaching things differently. "Recently, I saw myself getting defensive with Julia, so I gave her the option of finishing up the schedule. It was a concrete and symbolic letting go of that issue, trusting her."

Relationships with the Children

Persistent tension between their parents impacted Ivan and Julia's daughters. "Even now, they have told me they don't like to deal with deciding which house to go to when they come into town. It's this interesting juggle between figuring out which parent to be with and, most important, finding their friends."

Ivan enjoys a strong relationship with his daughters. "I can talk with them, there is trust and honesty. The older, Noreen, asks lots of questions.

Mona does, too, but she isn't so introspective. I see them watching me make this shift, living into a different life."

As Lyn did in the previous story, Ivan believes he was modelling good things. "I hope my kids are seeing how we all learn the balance between dependence and independence, how you trust without giving yourself up. I think they're doing a lot of sorting out. I hope they are learning that hanging in and doing the best you can is a good way to go."

Ivan and Julia used their self-management skills to achieve a smooth and co-operative separation. However, they got snagged in a power struggle about the amount of time each had with their girls, which proved hard to escape. Ivan also felt anger at how the legal system treated fathers. As he grew to understand himself better, Ivan learned to back away from the power struggle. His daughters developed good relationships with both parents. Ivan believed that they were absorbing good lessons from seeing him grow.

CASSIE'S STORY:
STAYING AFLOAT THROUGH TURBULENCE

shared expectations • helping daughter through anger • growth

"In the depths of winter, I found within me an invincible summer." Cassie's referencing of Albert Camus summed up her strong sense of growth after two years' separation from Neil. She and her daughter had both learned important things. At forty-three, Cassie had recently landed a new job, and her voice rang with relief and elation that she was on track for her future.

Cassie and Neil's daughter, Diane, was almost ten when Cassie and I met. The parents held shared expectations of co-parenting, which underpinned all that followed their split. "We both agreed that neither of us would take her away from the other. I wouldn't do that to Diane, and I wouldn't do that to Neil — it would be horrible." The parents found homes within ten minutes' drive of each other in Calgary.

Neil's work dictated most of their schedule, requiring fourteen-hour workdays every other week. Diane lived with Cassie during those weeks and with her dad the other weeks. "I could have been a jerk about that, but it wouldn't have served the greater good about neither of us taking her away. Actually, during the marriage, she hardly saw her dad during those long workday weeks, so it wasn't that functionally different." Neil and Cassie were flexible around who had Diane for school vacations, not worrying about having absolutely equal amounts of time with her.

Finances required the most discussion. Cassie noticed that talking specifics helped the parents reach agreement. "Neil's very rational, so when I'd say that Diane needs a raincoat of a certain quality every year that costs this much, it worked." They had been splitting costs 40-60, with Neil paying 60 percent, but expected to move soon to 50-50 thanks to Cassie's new job.

The parents had fairly similar styles of interacting with Diane, and Cassie felt comfortable that Diane was receiving sufficiently consistent care. Cassie's challenge was feeling in competition with Neil. "It's been hard not to worry that she likes him better than me ... I have some very competitive moments. For a while they seemed to be doing everything together, and whenever she came to my place it was kind of a downer. I felt like the loser parent. Now the tables have turned. She is excited about her new room in my new place." Cassie's self-management skills showed in her awareness of her own feelings.

Impacts on Diane

The separation triggered difficult behaviour in their daughter. "A few months in, she was clearly angry at both of us, and she had no place to take those feelings. She started throwing tantrums — it was every mother's nightmare. Then I talked with her dad, and it turned out she was an equal-opportunity tantrum-thrower!" Cassie grinned.

The parents took action. "We got her this great therapist, whom she worked with for a year and a half, and it got a little easier. She had a place to be mad and work out her other feelings, and just come home and be herself. Sometimes she would have specific things she wanted to talk about that we could both discuss with her." Diane's therapy not only got her through her distressing feelings, but also taught her new self-management skills. "Once she got past that anger, she just swung with it. She does different things with both of us, is getting good grades, and her social relationships are better as she's learned some good coping skills. She's a resilient, happy kid."

As other parents had observed, Cassie felt she had become a much better parent since divorcing. "The quality of the parenting she gets from both her dad and me has gone up. I have become more fully engaged with her. Knowing that I don't have that much time with her means I have really upped my game when she and I are together."

She felt good about all that Diane was learning. "Neil and I are such different people! He takes her on camping trips, while I won't sleep on the ground. I take her to Winners, and he sure doesn't want to do that. Somebody is covering all the bases for her. I think she has learned that women have options, and that marriage is only one choice — we can be happy in many choices."

Cassie's Journey

Cassie felt like she was riding a roller coaster for the first year post-separation. "I went back to school and to a new job, all at the same time. The first week I probably lost ten pounds, feeling so nervous and over-whelmed. I hadn't been working at someone else's business in ten years. The fluorescent lights in my office gave me a headache. I felt so sad — I thought my life was over! But I got a lamp for my office, and the work got interesting and school picked up. Things got so much better. Around Christmas, things got hard again. I wondered how we could do two celebrations with Diane." The next spring, Diane came to watch Cassie graduate from university. "That was a big high."

Support from friends and family helped Cassie enormously. Her self-management skills were already good, and she learned more. "I have this friend who was just patient; she let me sit in the dark and ruminate about my fears. She held me bigger than I held myself, yet didn't push me. She was a great friend in that respect. Others helped out in little ways that are huge — they would pick Diane up now and then, occasionally give her dinner. My brother has gotten much closer to my daughter; he wants to be helpful to me, and has become more of a kid person than before."

Cassie grew as a money earner, a parent, and a person. "I now believe that I can support myself and don't need Neil's money to make it. That's been a big change. My sense of myself as a parent has become stronger; I thought I was a pretty good parent, but now I know it! No one would have said before that I was not a confident person. But now, not only has my confidence increased, it has gone deeper. I knew I was strong, but I've learned that I'm tough, I can take a lot. I learned to let go of a lot of crap. You need to ask people to help you. That's a hard one for me — I can't stand asking for help. But I've gotten over that. You really can't do it all by yourself."

As other parents also observed, learning to accept what was in her control made Cassie's life easier. "It would have helped me to understand earlier that your ex-partner is never going to be different than who they are — this *is* who they are. And working with that isn't condoning anything, or giving in. Let go of the hope that she or he will change — they won't. And that's okay. You can still do a good job of parenting together."

Cassie and Neil held a similar view of co-parenting, and had good physical health and reasonable financial health. Cassie increased her self-management skills, learning to ask for help and to focus on things within her control. Her daughter, Diane, grew too, learning coping skills to deal with her anger. Their growth made life flow more easily for everyone.

LETITIA'S STORY: MAKING IT WORK

communication skills • using discipline together
ex's new partner

Thirty-one-year-old Letitia and her ex-husband, Brady, found a way to co-parent from a rocky start. Letitia sought lots of advice and support, and had learned much since her and Brady's separation five years before.

The Start of Co-Parenting

Letitia's parents divorced when she was small, and she'd had little contact with her father. "That shaped me. I didn't know how to deal with men in authority or men in my relationships." While married to Brady, she found him intimidating and verbally abusive. They tried marriage counselling, but when Letitia was twenty-six, Brady asked for a divorce. Letitia knew right away she wanted their eleven-month-old daughter, Kyla, to have both parents in her life. She was determined that Kyla wouldn't repeat her own experience of fatherlessness.

Letitia felt alone and distraught after the split. She lived in California, working as an events coordinator, and missed her family in New Hampshire, too far away to give her much support. She was the first of her friends to marry and have children.

She took training in anger management and found a course for people who were either perpetrators or victims of domestic violence. "The ALIVE program basically taught you how not to be a victim and about the roles people play. We divided the roles into feminine and masculine roles. We talked about masculine words like *patronizing* and *king*, and feminine words like *doormat*. We learned that just because we've been assigned these roles, we don't have to keep them. I was able to figure out my own relationship dynamics and start reacting differently."

Letitia's learning shifted her perspective and gave her new skills. "I learned not to blame Brady for things. He intimidated the heck out of me — things were always my fault, and he was patronizing. I learned not to use blame, like 'you did this, you did that,' and say, 'I felt … when you did….' I tried to use that in the mediation and it really helped. Even today, I need to remember that Brady does this and I need to not react, and communicate differently."

Afraid of losing Kyla, she hired a lawyer and researched parenting plans. The parents went to mediation. With their communication working better, they found they shared expectations around co-parenting and agreed on a plan drafted by Letitia. "The mediator said it was the best thing she had ever seen. That felt awesome."

They co-parented for two years on a fifty-fifty schedule. After Brady moved from Sacramento to San Francisco when Kyla was four, Letitia followed one year later, driving back and forth in the meantime. "I was happy in Sacramento, but I didn't want to go to court and make the judge choose between us. We're both really good parents. Finally my work was able to transfer me last year. Kyla started kindergarten last September and things are easier."

Letitia liked the shared schedule. "I'm really busy at work, so it's great to have a week when I can concentrate on that and travel for work on my week off. I don't do anything socially when I don't have Kyla, but I could. It gives me a break. Sometimes you just need a couple of hours."

Parenting from Two Homes

While Letitia and Brady found a way to work together, they had to tackle new problems that arose, such as discipline. "At this year's parent-teacher conference, the teacher said that Kyla was a little rough. A lot of kids didn't want to play with her because she hit them and wouldn't respect it if they said no to her; she just kept doing whatever she was doing."

The parents discussed discipline for the first time. Letitia acknowledged that Kyla was getting mixed messages through their different discipline styles. "I haven't been consistent with her, and I should have been. She's really a good kid."

Letitia bought children's books on how to be a good friend to read with Kyla. Brady set up a reward system at his house. Letitia believed she should implement the same system in her home, but was still figuring out how to do it.

Since Letitia and Brady shared time equally, support payments weren't an issue. "I care more about school and he cares more about sports. He's willing to pay more in that area. We'll keep having to sort that out."

Accepting New Realities

Brady's new partner, Lee, raised Letitia's hackles. "Lee came with Brady to the preschool teacher meeting. I was really upset. Then Brady told Kyla she could call Lee 'Momma Lee,' and that really bothered me, like some boundaries were crossed."

She reached for an outside perspective. "I talked to a friend who was dating someone with two older children. My friend would help the kids with their homework; she loved them. She reminded me that it's better if the girlfriend cares about your child. As long as Kyla knows that I'm her mom, that's fine."

Letitia gradually accepted that Lee was in the picture. Her growing comfort with Lee made everyone more relaxed. "For Kyla's fifth birthday, I planned the party myself. Brady was there with Lee. My single mom friends were shocked, saying, 'Oh my god, she's hugging Kyla and you're okay with that.' They were surprised that I wasn't mad."

When Kyla turned six, Letitia, Brady, and Lee planned the birthday party together. Letitia thought back to their separation, when she had dreamed of being able to plan and hold a birthday party together. "I'm glad to be where we are today. It has surprised me how Brady has changed. I think his girlfriend's been a really good influence because she had a child, and if she said something, he would listen. He seemed to be more flexible on some things. Now he's really supportive."

Impacts on Kyla

"The separation is all Kyla has known. We both meet our daughter's needs because we're different. I pay more attention to serious things like school; her dad pays more attention to sports and fun stuff. She gets a balance from us. We went to baseball tryouts together last year, and she is always happy when we do things together with her."

Letitia's Growth

Letitia continued to find supports that taught and sustained her. "I've turned to books for advice, and used the online community. The blog *SingleMommyHood* gave me good tips and perspectives from others' experiences. A friend from work brought us into her family for Thanksgiving dinner. It helped."

Letitia learned about trust and letting go. "When Kyla was three, my ex was working as a gymnastics coach and brought Kyla with him. I really worried about that. My friend said, 'Guys and girls parent differently and you have to trust that he is looking after her.' She taught me that you can't control people. That was really hard, a major lesson — letting go of control, increasing the trust."

Letitia's decision-making skills improved. "I am able to assess more of what I am looking for in a relationship. I know what I don't want. I need to focus a bit more on myself, move on with my life, and not worry about his."

She felt new pride. "My friends have told me they're amazed at how strong I am. I'm like, really? I didn't think I was that strong until I went through this, and now I recognize it. A friend who's leaving her husband is asking me for advice now. Wow."

Letitia was thinking of getting a master's degree in counselling so she could work with divorcing parents as a mediator. "I'm not sure, though, if I want to go back to school and start over again at thirty-one."

Brady and Letitia initially had many communication problems, yet their respect for each other as parents allowed them to agree on a shared schedule. Letitia increased her self-management skills in many ways: accepting differences, getting comfortable with Brady's new girlfriend, loosening control, and gaining confidence. Complicated, important stuff. As a result, Kyla received lots of love and attention in her two homes as her parents worked together.

JOE'S STORY:
GROWING AS A FATHER AND A MAN

learning to be a dad • expanding as a person

Remember Joe, from Joe and Sandy's stories in Chapter 2? This couple lived an inspiring path in which they tried living upstairs and downstairs in the same house, then lived separately, and three years later all moved into a new house, co-parenting with each other and Sandy's new female partner. Joe had so many insightful comments about how he grew that I saved some of them for this chapter.

He described what had built his confidence as a dad. "One of the things I did socially was canoeing every Wednesday. Before I had a place where I could bring the kids overnight, I took them camping for four or five weekends. I canoed out with all three of them and the tent, and camped on the river."

He learned from the intensity and the responsibility. "Those were really special times. I felt a little nervous being out there with the kids overnight by myself. It was isolated. I realized that as the parent, I had to be calm and cool. Even when we paddled out and I'd forgotten the tent and we had to paddle back in the dark to get it, I had to stay cool so they wouldn't get scared. I learned how to be more for the kids."

"I grew a lot that summer as a dad, I think. I had never had that one-on-one time with them. I started to see being a parent in a different way, and things began expanding for me. But it took a while, it didn't happen at once."

He found more room to be himself. "I felt like I was actively parenting. While married, my style was more passive than Sandy's really strong personality — I went with the flow. Being on my own re-established my own identity, my own life. And not always in a smooth, graceful way! Sometimes I was abrupt, like when I told Sandy, 'This is my time. They will be safe and have fun, but we are going to do things my way.'" He laughed. "I stumbled and fell a bit, and felt more like I could do things. Not just parenting but making life decisions. I had deferred so many things throughout the marriage. This increased my confidence."

Joe's canoe camping in the wilderness led him to more active and confident parenting. He grew in meeting his children's needs. Living single allowed him to see the drawbacks of his style of going with the flow, and he understood himself more fully. His growth made him a better parent, helped him share parenting with Sandy more easily, and helped their children thrive.

KRISTIN'S STORY:
CATALYST FOR GROWTH

careful decision-making • shared goals
learning independence

A relaxed and confident fifty-year-old, Kristin spoke comfortably about her changes and her resulting growth. She had navigated a contentious divorce, financial uncertainty, and worry about her children. She was now content with her decisions and how her sons were turning out.

When her marriage ended thirteen years earlier, Kristin wasn't a very independent person and didn't know herself well. The increased responsibilities of separation acted as a catalyst. "It was all up to me, there was no one else to blame. It was liberating! I changed in many ways, like my appearance. I grew my hair long for the first time and started to think about how I looked. This gave me confidence to meet new people."

Kristin had spent the six years prior to separation at home full-time; her sons were six and eight years old. Kristin's husband, Ron, wanted full custody of their children. With the help of her counsellor, Kristin looked at her options and the possible outcomes of a court battle. She decided that if she played hardball and their father lost, he would likely flee to another country and be gone from the children altogether — a horrifying prospect. Instead, she asked herself what she needed and what would work for the children. She concluded that fifty-fifty parenting was feasible.

Negotiations began tensely. "We started with accusations and out-rageous demands. I stood my ground most of the time. We did some mediation, which was free. He wanted to get lawyers involved, so we did. When he realized I wasn't trying to take everything from him, he was easier to deal with."

Kristin's situation was made easier, though it didn't feel so at the time, by her confidence in Ron as a father. She believed that fifty-fifty parenting would be best for the boys and keep them feeling most like a family.

Finalizing a plan was still challenging. She told Ron she wanted him to be in the children's lives. "It took a lot of patience and remembering what I wanted in the end. I bit my tongue many times." To avoid corrosive haggling about the house, she accepted one-third of the house's value, which was enough to let her rent a townhouse. Her friends told her she was crazy, but Kristin knew that it was more important for her to maintain good relations with Ron than to go after perfectly equal shares, as long as she had enough money to be healthy.

"It was such a relief when we reached the agreement. No more fights, no more money going out. I could get on with my life."

Living the Co-Parent Agreement

Once Kristin had rented a house, the kids lived week-on/week-off with each parent. Constant worry about money and whether she could make everything work took its toll. "It was scary, lonely, and exhilarating. When I signed the contract for the townhouse, I felt, 'I can do this!' Yet I was exhausted and had occasional meltdowns. One day the kids were painting little toys on the kitchen table. Seven-year-old Tony jostled a couple of tins of paint and spilled them — it turned out they were oil-based! — and I lost it." Stress and uncertainty persisted for several years, causing her to lose weight.

Even with the financial strain, Kristin believed that she had made good choices. "I did my best for the boys. Nothing in their lives stopped because of the split."

Because Kristin and Ron shared goals for parenting, they could talk easily about how their kids were doing. Kristin saw Ron as a wonderful dad, stricter than she was. "The kids have a really good work ethic because of him. Between us, we have a balance." She knew that all parents didn't work together the way they had. "I've listened to horror stories — am I lucky!"

Kristin stayed single for six years and felt her lack of a partner keenly. "Doing it with no one to support me was tough. I couldn't plan my future, even see my future. I couldn't imagine getting to the point of going on vacation — anything beyond next week! My goal was just to function. I missed company at night; I like to go for a walk, but had no one to walk with."

To cope with her loneliness, she kept a diary for the first time. "It was cathartic! I wrote down what I was feeling. Writing seemed to help — it gave me clarity and made it easier to see what to do next."

Thirteen Years Later

The children, seventeen and twenty at interview time, were doing well. "They had easy access to us both. They kept the same school, and life was as normal as possible. They hated having to pack up their stuff to shift houses, at the beginning. Later on, they seemed to like getting away from their dad for a while (probably the same with me). Now I'm really proud of them. They are down-to-earth, nice people."

The best part of co-parenting for Kristin was growing. "I am more mature now. In my current relationship, I stand up for myself and ask for what I want. I feel I deserve to be heard and have the things that I need. My self-confidence has grown so much, I know I can do anything I want to do. I never was tested before — you have to be tested. I am self-reliant."

Her advice to her earlier self: "Don't worry. Some good things will come out of all this. You'll become a stronger, better person. Try to make sure the kids don't worry about Mom and Dad."

Here is another example of parents with respect for each other and significant self-management skills. The struggle around parenting time still wasn't easy, though. Kristin's thoughtful decision-making, supported by counselling, paid off. It was important to her that Ron was part of their sons' lives, and she accepted the price of short-term stresses to help that happen. Her pleasure in how the boys turned out matched her deep joy at discovering her own strength.

What Do These Stories Tell Us?

These parents began with varying levels of self-management skills. Some shared similar expectations with their ex-spouses on parenting, while others did not and needed to negotiate. As each parent gained self-understanding, they were able to act more flexibly. Angela reached for supports, which helped her grow in confidence and maintain a close relationship with her children, though her finances remained worrisome.

Lyn and Linc took their time in physically separating to minimize the impact on their children. Lyn saw her sons thriving in a different family pattern, and learned she could succeed in owning and managing her own house. She grew in self-confidence through acting on her values.

Ivan and Julia's high self-management skills let them separate smoothly, but they became trapped in a power struggle over the time split with their daughters. Ivan sought lots of assistance to grow, and learned to draw back and focus more on living his own life. Their children reaped the benefits of parents who communicated clearly, saw others' viewpoints, and made decisions that took others' needs into account.

> Developing good self-management skills and surviving challenges results in increased self-confidence.

Cassie had financial and emotional challenges, although she and her ex shared a picture of co-parenting. Cassie hadn't supported herself before separating and had to discover that she could. She learned to ask for help, and her daughter, Diane, developed skills for handling her anger.

Letitia's separation sparked huge growth as she gained new perspectives on how to avoid blaming while talking with her ex, Brady. Through courses, counselling, and friends, she learned to let go, accept Brady's girlfriend, and co-parent in a way that their daughter felt she was loved by many.

Joe grew in taking a full father role. Spending time with his children let him see what they needed from him. Making his own choices and learning from the results allowed him to become a steady, flexible man.

Kristin used counselling to help achieve her goal of shared parenting. She accepted an uneven financial split in divorcing in order to avoid conflict. This led to stressful years for her, but she believed her decisions had paid off for her children.

Good self-management skills did not banish the loneliness of shifting to a single life felt by many mothers and fathers. Surviving that pain and finding ways to ease it helped parents learn to trust themselves. As they made good decisions, stayed afloat financially and emotionally, and learned to be there for their children, they developed confidence that they could make things work — a precious feeling for anyone. Parents with this gut faith in themselves believed they had become better parents. They lived in a more relaxed, confident, and loving way with their children and their world.

12 Quick Pointers: What Helped?

Character is made in the small moments of our lives.
— PHILLIPS BROOKS

We have seen principles that help co-parents: keep the children's interests central, accept reality, take time to make decisions, focus on what you can control, and nurture yourself so you keep growing. These are broad ideas to keep in mind. Parents also reported many specific actions that made things work better. They are listed below, with examples from stories, so if you want to check back for the context of that action, you know where to look.

What Parents Can Do

1. **Choose where you seek support.**

   Parents valued having friends or family who would listen to them vent and give non-judgmental support. This was most helpful when it included neutrality about their ex-partner. Choose who you unload on. Having a friend listen to you rail about your ex is one thing; having them support you in demonizing your ex is quite another. Friends who leap in to build up your sense of being wronged may provoke you into intensifying conflict.

   Pauline, Chapter 3: "Before, I used to eat, call my parents, and cry to them." Her father gently pointed out that she was putting herself under stress and therefore could do something to change it. This encouraged her to look for new options, like exercising, to relieve her anxiety.

Carter, Chapter 10: "Don't badmouth your ex or her family; be respectful; be supportive." His father's advice made him carefully consider his decisions.

2. **Find ways to let feelings go.**
   Journal writing can be a safe place to vent and explore feelings.

   Gloria, Chapter 2: "I wrote everything down. At one point I even made a book of our relationship, to get everything in perspective. Blogging on open forums helped; even if no one was listening, it felt like someone was."

   Kristin, Chapter 11: "It was cathartic! I wrote down what I was feeling. Writing seemed to help — it gave me clarity and made it easier to see what to do next."

   Other methods work, too: exercise, creative projects, and therapy or counselling.

   Pauline, Chapter 3: "I would go home and stuff myself. Then I went back to school, began exercising, and started my business. Now I tell myself, 'I'm going to love my children more than I hate my ex, and walk on the treadmill.' Sometimes I'm on it for an hour and I don't realize it, I just need to walk it off." Pauline replaced eating with exercising as a way to release her anger.

   Francesca, Chapter 4: She used two counsellors. "I really took time to understand myself. I knew I would want to be in a relationship again, and I didn't want to be bitter or angry. I wanted a more positive, whole relationship."

   Janice, Chapter 5: "I sing, and write songs, that's a healing thing." She let her feelings emerge in private when she didn't need to take care of anyone else.

3. **Learn to handle conflict skillfully.**
   Be specific. Decide what you want to say ahead of time, and choose exactly what points you want to make, rather than making broad statements. This tactic will help keep discussions on track.

   Cassie, Chapter 11: Finances required the most discussion. Cassie noticed that talking specifics helped the parents reach agreement.

"Neil's very rational, so when I'd say that Diane needs a raincoat of a certain quality every year that costs this much, it worked."

4. **Focus on your own vegetable patch.**
What? No, this isn't about carrots and turnips. Unless there is an issue of physical safety or mental health, accept that the other parent will raise the children as they see fit. Again, it's about accepting what we can control and what we cannot.

When *Gloria*, in *Chapter 2*, learned to stop trying to control Janey's life with Fred, he in turn was able to be open enough to learn from the judge's blunt remarks to him about how much Gloria was giving up. The relationship between the parents improved, and Janey gained two parents who were able to work together for her.

5. **Know you are a model.**
Our children are always watching us, seeing how we respond and how we make things happen.

Cassie, Chapter 11: "I think she has learned that women have options, and that marriage is only one choice — we can be happy in many choices." She modelled her belief that there are many paths to a successful life.

Janice, Chapter 5: "Watching Mom be passionate and work hard — that's empowering for kids. Not seeing me trampled down." She believed that it strengthened Kelly to see her mother acting in a powerful way.

6. **Change living arrangements with care.**
How you make the first transition to two households is important. Telling the children what to expect ahead of time, and involving them where possible, gives them some sense of control and predictability.

Veronica, Chapter 10: She planned the shift from one home to two with Stanley. Following their counsellor's advice, they prepared the new apartment before telling their children of the split. Then, all four went to view the new place and discuss which furniture would stay in the original home and which would go to the new apartment. Veronica felt that their sons accepted the separation pretty well.

7. **If parenting from a distance, find ways to be part of your child's life.**
Fun outings are great but not enough. By joining in some of your child's regular activities and social connections, you will develop and keep a deeper bond.

Stefan, Chapter 2: He volunteered at Ben's school, so each Friday of his long weekends in Kansas he would be in the classroom, supporting the teacher. This gave him a chance not only to interact with Ben, but also to see him with his classmates and get to know them, too.

8. **Explain choices to children.**
Our children see the results of our many choices, but they have no way to understand our reasons for making them unless we tell them.

As *Lyn*, in *Chapter 11*, explained to her boys, "I'm not saying this to make you feel bad, but I want you to know that I made a choice. I wanted to own a property here in Seattle, and so I can't provide these things like Jet Skis for you right now." They responded well to learning her reasons. (**Warning**: this can be a tricky one. Make sure that if you plan to explain a choice, you won't be subtly undermining or complaining about your ex as you do so. Keep it simple and matter-of-fact.)

9. **Introduce new partners carefully.**
New partners can be a minefield, with children feeling divided loyalties and confusion. Agreeing on a way to consciously bring in new partners can ease the way for the adults and the children.

Ayla, Chapter 10: She and Andrew agreed that neither would have the children meet any new romantic partner until the relationship was serious. At that point, the new partner would meet the other parent (the ex) before the kids did. Bettina, the new stepmom of Ayla's kids, told Ayla that she didn't think she would have been accepted so well if Ayla had been neutral in referring to her. Instead, Ayla had said, "I've met Bettina, I think she's really nice." Ayla commented, "We gave them permission to develop a relationship with the new person with no worries."

This important strategy requires accepting the reality of your ex's new partner. If this is hard, remember that your children will benefit from your generosity of spirit.

10. **Find new interests.**

This may sound like a line from a magazine article, but it feels great to find ways to nurture and expand yourself.

Angela, Chapter 11: In the midst of gruelling negotiations with her ex-husband, Angela signed up for salsa lessons. "The joy from dancing was exquisite. You're moving to music and it's wonderful. I felt feminine, attractive, worth a million bucks." The dancing challenged her mind and body.

11. **Find online resources.**

Letitia, Chapter 11: "The blog *SingleMommyHood* gave me good tips and perspectives from others' experiences."

Elaine, Chapter 9: Elaine discovered an online site, Our Family Wizard, which included a shared calendar and places to record expenses. Tracking what each parent spent got them away from the "I'm paying more" issue. Over time, they saw that they were paying about the same. That helped.

What Friends and Family Can Do

1. **Offer financial help.**

Offers of loans or money for legal bills were mentioned frequently and with gratitude. These made parents feel that they were not totally alone, that others nearby cared enough to prop them up in particular ways, from time to time.

2. **Act like extended family.**

   Letitia, Chapter 11: "A friend from work brought us into her family for Thanksgiving dinner. It helped."

   Angela, Chapter 11: "I had a sweetheart of a friend who lived two doors down. The summer my husband moved out, she stopped by every few days. She would knock at the door and call, 'Just checking in.' It meant so much to me."

   Small acts can greatly reduce loneliness and isolation.

3. **Show appreciation of parenting.**

   Co-parents often feel that they are blazing a trail, and wonder if they are doing it right. Reassurance makes a huge difference.

   Ayla, Chapter 10: "Friends were encouraging and complimentary about how we were handling the co-parenting. They saw the kids being happy; this validation meant a lot."

4. **Listen, remind parents of who they are, and believe in their capacity.**

   Cassie, Chapter 11: "I have this friend who was just patient; she let me sit in the dark and ruminate about my fears. She held me bigger than I held myself, yet didn't push me."

   Elaine, Chapter 9: "My friends lifted and held me by hearing me vent, offering perspectives, and reiterating my value in the world. Spending time with those who had known me before as well as after my life with Greta made me feel safe. My friends saw me wounded and disabled, and stayed with me to help me become able again."

   A friend can be a life preserver and even a mentor.

5. **Be the intermediate place if needed.**

   Sometimes conflict between co-parents is intractable. Minimizing face-to-face encounters can decrease conflict and tensions. Grandparents who act as a go-between develop deeper relationships with their grandchildren.

   Carmela, Chapter 4: Carmela's mother received the baby from each parent and gave him to the other parent. This let the mother and father avoid direct contact when conflict was likely to erupt if they came face-to-face.

6. **Build emotional bridges.**
Brett, Chapter 4: Brett's sister, when visiting, was able to reopen communication between Brett and his older daughter. Aunts, uncles, and grandparents can sometimes gently use their relationship to nudge older children (or adults) to re-examine their reactions.

7. **Make travel between parents easier.**
Whatever will support the logistics of children travelling between two homes is invaluable. It can reduce financial strain on the parents by enabling commuting, and ease children's sense of dislocation.

My story, Chapter 1: "To our delight, when the fence was completed, we saw that the neighbour had built in a tiny child-sized door just for the boys! This family had taken our unique circumstance into account and gone to extra trouble and expense to help us."

Carter, Chapter 10: One parent would drop Sandra off at Grandma's house. The grandmother took her to school and picked her up, with the other parent picking Sandra up after work if it was a changeover day. This meant that the parents could live some distance from each other and still have a feasible schedule for Sandra. It also meant that Sandra's grandmother could be part of her granddaughter's life.

8. **Do things the other parent would do.**
Wanda, Chapter 9: Friends helped in practical ways, bringing Wanda a birthday gift from Zoe when she was too young to buy it herself. They did things that the other parent would do in an intact family, and it made a big difference to Wanda.

Small acts, like helping a child pick out a card for the parent, can make the parent feel less alone.

What Institutions Can Do

1. **Prepare a binder for each parent for meetings.**

    Concrete recognition of family structure reduces awkward fumbling by the co-parents and helps them feel normal.

    Wanda, Chapter 9: Zoe's school recognized her family's unique structure by having a binder ready for each mother at the school orientation.

2. **Foster the individual's personal growth.**

    There are countless people who form part of the family's social and professional sphere: teachers, child care workers, doctors and clinic personnel, mediators, babysitters, and more. Take comfort knowing that children and parents benefit from your skillful support, whether you can see it or not.

13 Twelve Things Learned

You gain strength, courage, and confidence by every experience for which you must stop and look fear in the face. You must do the thing you think you cannot do.

— ELEANOR ROOSEVELT

Each morning you wake up to your own life and no one else's. Whether you can't wait to spring out of bed or want to huddle under the covers forever, you still have to *be* in your situation every day. You can't resign from your life like you can from a job. Many mothers and fathers in these stories faced daunting circumstances as they began co-parenting. Armed with whatever physical health, financial means, and inner resources they possessed right then, they acted. The paths they created were not always ideal, yet they did keep going. Sometimes they shaped new and inspiring realities.

So what? What do the stories show? Here are twelve insights that stood out for me:

1. **It gets easier.**
   Some of the ease comes with learning that you survive. A massive shift can make you hold your breath, as if you have jumped into cold water. You aren't sure that you'll make it through. With time, you get used to the new temperature. You learn you can still breathe. You can not only tread water, but swim forward.

2. **It's not just about getting over the divorce.**

Getting through the divorce is only the first part of the job. Instead of this being a one-time task, with steps you accomplish and are done with, you may need to deal with waves of change for the next decade. If your former spouse takes actions like disparaging you, moving without notice, or being inconsistent in following agreements, you will likely feel ongoing anger and uncertainty. Use and strengthen your self-management skills, take care of yourself, and stay focused on the children's needs.

3. **Face your feelings.**

This may be the first time you've experienced such powerful emotions. You may not know how to stay with them. Don't ignore or push away your feelings — or not for long — or you risk staying stuck in pain. Instead, give attention to whatever you feel about the divorce and your changing life. Accept that the feelings can be painful, and seek help, if needed, from counsellors, therapists, books, or support groups. If the marriage's end echoes events from your past, there may be leftover guilt or sadness needing extra attention. If you stay in tune with your own feelings, you will more likely sense your children's feelings as well. You'll know if they need help.

4. **Stronger parents mean stronger kids.**

Rising to the demands of co-parenting created new perspectives, skills, and confidence in almost all parents interviewed. Mothers' and fathers' development strengthened their parenting, and the children reaped the benefits of parents who were more confident in themselves and present for their kids. Your growth supports your children's growth.

5. **No one regretted getting help.**

Many parents wished they had done some things differently. They felt bad that they had made poor decisions or hadn't seen warning signs in time. But no one was sorry for getting support from counsellors, coaches, financial advisers, support groups, massage therapists — whoever would bolster their inner resources. Even if it's not comfortable, consider seriously your options for strengthening yourself in decision-making, acknowledging feelings, education, or getting along with others. There are countless resources, so give some a try. It won't hurt, and it may make a difference for you and your children. Do whatever will nourish and expand you. This is one area where you have some control.

6. **Seeing the big picture makes a big difference.**
   Remember Chapter 2? The big picture included financial, mental, and physical health, as well as self-management skills and shared expectations. Even when both parents have high levels of self-management skills and similar expectations, co-parenting is challenging. When extra stressors are present, particularly special needs of a child or parent, or addictions, everyone involved needs to invest more ongoing energy. If this is your situation, accept that you will need support: ask for help and keep seeking whatever will enable you to keep going. If this is the situation of someone close to you, offer whatever support you can.

7. **Co-parenting is dynamic.**
   Your work situation changes; your ex-spouse needs to move; another child arrives; your children need different things from you and their other parent as they mature. Co-parenting may work with parents sharing time equally for two years, or eight years. At other times, one parent may have most of the time with the children. Expect changes and shifts.

8. **Take time to make good decisions.**
   You can't know what's going to happen, but you have to make decisions that will impact the future anyway. It is important to take time to explore and test your assumptions about what will be best for you and your children. Your anger, hurt, or fear can be so strong that stepping back to get more perspective is the last thing you want to

do. It's still important. This is particularly true in the first two years post-split, when it is hardest to see the children's needs as distinct from your own.

9. **Avoid drama, if you can.**
Some high-conflict stories included dramatic actions, like throwing the partner's belongings outside or having loud arguments that the children could hear. Anger can be a valuable force that moves you to action, yet its unfiltered expression can also leave scars. While sometimes unavoidable, each dramatic action has the potential to escalate conflict. The more frequently open conflict occurs, the more it can impact your children, leaving them with memories they want to forget.

10. **Learn forgiveness.**
No one parents, or co-parents, perfectly. Carrying blame and shame in your heart keeps you anchored in the past. Divorce brings intense feelings, and no one is at their best when navigating those shoals of hurt and anger. Notice when you screw up, and think about how to avoid doing that again. Then remember how many things you are doing right, and forgive yourself. If possible, with time (perhaps lots of time!), try to forgive your ex, too. You will feel lighter.

11. **Nobody knows what's next.**
You *want* so much to feel a sense of control or predictability where your children are concerned. Remember that not all unexpected events will be bad. Out of the blue, some shifts will improve your kids' lives, your relationship with your ex, your career prospects — whatever. So when you gaze ahead into the uncertain future, try not to keep yourself only braced for hard things. Make sure to leave mental room for some good surprises, too.

12. **Hope is important.**
    As long as you believe that better things are possible, you can keep going.

What to Hope For?

In hearing these stories so generously shared, I wondered, *What is a reasonable outcome to hope for as a co-parent?* Given the vast breadth of starting points, no one path or outcome will make sense. My best answer is that

- the children's physical and mental needs are met as they grow and change;
- the parent finds a way to keep moving forward;
- each child has an enduring relationship with both parents, with the chance to know and understand their gifts and flaws; and
- the parent is able to grow, however he or she defines that: in self-management skills, career, health, stability, relationships.

What is your answer?

I shall either find a way or make one.
— ELEANOR ROOSEVELT

Acknowledgements

A deep bow to all those who shared their experiences in these interviews. Thank you for your time, openness, and generosity.

To the many who helped me sort through ideas and search for co-parents: Leigh Bowie, Roq Gareau, Lorraine Hand, Ken Kristjanson, Edward Kruk, Leading Women for Shared Parenting, Carey Linde, Gladys Loewen, Janet Mairs, Deesha Philyaw, Meg Salter, Audrey Sutton, Lorraine Sutton, Lorraine Wright, and others.

To the many who helped me write and believed that I could: the Port Moody Writers' Group, including Julie, Anyes, Liz, Anita, Debra, Deborah, Patti, Mona, Claire, and Mallee. The Rogue Writers Kathy and Michelle. Fellow writers on the path, Robert Burcher, Jill Malleck, Wendy Soe-lin, and Suzanne Tremblay. The White Rock Writers; beta readers Michelle, Judy, and Jim; my Rock of Gibraltar, editor Joyce Gram; and Julie Ferguson for all her wisdom.

To Bruce for your generous patience and loving support.

APPENDIX 1

Interview Details

Forty-two parents living in Canada or the U.S. were interviewed. Twenty-eight were mothers and fourteen were fathers. The majority lived in the western half of Canada and the northwest U.S. All were English-speaking. Ages ranged from late twenties to early sixties.

For most of the interviews, only one parent took part. Therefore, only that person's view of themselves, the marriage breakdown and parenting negotiations, impacts on children, and the other parent was available. I accepted everything said at face value, appreciating people's generosity and sincerity in making their experiences transparent in order to help others. At the same time, none of us is completely objective about ourselves — even less about our former spouses! So the interviews present an array of mostly partial views of co-parenting.

Not all interviews completed are included in this book. I selected a range to cover as wide a spectrum of situations and approaches as possible, and avoided using closely similar stories.

Interview Questions
Because circumstances, including ages of the children and length of time since separation, varied so much, not all questions applied for every parent.

1. Your situation now? How long since separation? Since divorce?
2. Think back and remember how things were before the marriage ended. How did you start to consider this parenting arrangement?

3. What factors played into your decision? Did either pressure or support from peers influence you?
4. How did you feel when thinking of co-parenting as an option?
5. What unanswered questions did you have?
6. What were the early stages of co-parenting like for you?
7. What were your feelings, thoughts, impulses, regrets?
8. Do any images or stories stand out particularly for you? Awkwardness? Joys?
9. In what ways did the new arrangement meet your needs? Your children's needs?
10. How did you arrive at a workable, shared agreement? What did doing this require of you?
11. How did it feel to have reached a workable agreement?
12. What were your goals in shared parenting? To what extent were they realized?
13. What was hardest for you? Hardest for the children?
14. Best parts for you? Best parts for them?
15. How did your sense of yourself as a person evolve? What did you learn about yourself? As a parent?
16. Did you have ongoing feelings of anger or other emotions at the other parent regarding how they were co-parenting? If so, how did you handle it? How did it, and does it, impact you?
17. What helpful roles did others play, such as extended family? Friends?
18. Are there things you wish you had been better at doing?
19. Did your level of ease in dealing with the other parent change over time? If so, in what ways? What contributed to that?
20. Who were the people who were the most significant for the children?
21. Where did your support come from?
22. What role have financial concerns played in your co-parenting?
23. Do any really great moments or situations stand out for you?
24. What was the most positive effect for your children from co-parenting?
25. How have the skills or strengths you accessed or developed through co-parenting showed up in other aspects of your life?

26. If you could go back in time to the beginning of divorce planning and give advice to the person you were, what would you say?
27. Anything else?

Methodology

I took written notes on all interviews, and recorded most, as well. In analyzing the responses from the interviews, I did not begin with a theory to test the data against. Instead, in the tradition of grounded research, I read and reread the answers, letting themes and patterns emerge gradually.

Self-Assessment of Skills for Co-Parenting

More self-management skills can make co-parenting easier; fewer skills make it harder. Below are specific skills that assist parents in developing a post-divorce relationship of working together in a businesslike way, regardless of feelings.

You can use the list below to assess your current levels. In which of these skills are you confident? Are there others that you struggle with regularly? How likely are you to do these things successfully in inter-actions with your former spouse or partner?

Co-Parenting Skills List

1. Detach and step back from intense discussions when feelings threaten to overwhelm.

   no chance   can do sometimes   do often   no problem

2. Use neutral language in discussions with former spouse and about former spouse.

   no chance   can do sometimes   do often   no problem

3. Think clearly about the steps needed to move forward.

   no chance   can do sometimes   do often   no problem

4. Articulate to former spouse your view of what is needed and what you are willing to do and not willing to do.

    no chance   *can do sometimes*   *do often*   *no problem*

5. Negotiate differences.

    no chance   *can do sometimes*   *do often*   *no problem*

6. Refrain from communicating through the children to their other parent.

    no chance   *can do sometimes*   *do often*   *no problem*

7. Obtain more information or support when needed to make a decision or when at an impasse.

    no chance   *can do sometimes*   *do often*   *no problem*

These skills and actions can be difficult in the early stages post-divorce. If some remain hard for you, remember how others have benefited from support, and get help.

APPENDIX 3

Resources

Co-Parenting

Avirat. Our Family Wizard. Accessed July 16, 2015. www.ourfamilywizard. com.

Burrett, Jill, and Michael Green. *Shared Parenting: Raising Your Children Cooperatively After Separation.* Berkeley: Celestial Arts, 2009.

Emery, Robert. *The Truth About Children and Divorce: Dealing with the Emotions So You and Your Children Can Thrive.* New York: Viking, 2004.

Kruk, Edward. *The Equal Parent Presumption: Social Justice in the Legal Determination of Parenting After Divorce.* Montreal & Kingston: McGill-Queen's University Press, 2013.

Mountain Dreamer, Oriah. *The Dance: Moving to the Rhythms of Your True Self.* Toronto: HarperCollins, 2001.

Osborne, Judy. *Wisdom for Separated Parents: Rearranging Around the Children to Keep Kinship Strong.* Santa Barbara: Praeger, 2011.

Philyaw, Deesha, and Michael Thomas. *Co-parenting 101: Helping Your Kids Thrive in Two Households After Divorce.* Oakland: New Harbinger Publications, 2013.

Ricci, Isolina. *Mom's House, Dad's House: Making Two Homes for Your Child.* New York: Fireside, 1997.

Ross, Julie, and Judy Corcoran. *Joint Custody with a Jerk: Raising a Child with an Uncooperative Ex: A Hands-on, Practical Guide to Communicating with a Difficult Ex-Spouse.* Rev. ed. New York: St. Martin's Griffin, 2011.

Royko, David. *Voices of Children of Divorce.* New York: Golden Books, 1999.

Thayer, Elizabeth, and Jeffrey Zimmerman. *The Co-Parenting Survival Guide: Letting Go of Conflict After a Difficult Divorce.* Oakland: New Harbinger Publications, 2001.

Wallerstein, Judith, Julia Lewis, and Sandra Blakeslee. *The Unexpected Legacy of Divorce: The 25 Year Landmark Study.* New York: Hyperion, 2000.

Personal Growth

Arrien, Angeles. *The Four-Fold Way: Walking the Paths of Warrior, Teacher, Healer and Visionary.* New York: HarperCollins, 1993.

Brown, Brené. *Daring Greatly: How the Courage To Be Vulnerable Transforms the Way We Live, Love, Parent, and Lead.* New York: Gotham Books, 2012.

Chödrön, Pema. *The Places That Scare You: A Guide to Fearlessness in Difficult Times.* Boston: Shambhala, 2002.

———. *Start Where You Are: A Guide to Compassionate Living.* Boston: Shambhala, 2004.

Irvine, David. *Becoming Real: Journey to Authenticity.* Sanford, FL: DC Press, 2003.

Kabat-Zinn, Jon. *Full Catastrophe Living: Using the Wisdom of Your Body and Mind to Face Stress, Pain, and Illness.* New York: Bantam Dell, 1990.

Lerner, Harriet G. *The Dance of Deception: Pretending and Truth-Telling in Women's Lives.* New York: HarperCollins, 1993.

Mountain Dreamer, Oriah. *The Dance: Moving to the Rhythms of Your True Self.* Toronto: HarperCollins, 2002.

Myss, Caroline. *Anatomy of the Spirit: The Seven Stages of Power and Healing.* New York: Three Rivers Press, 1996.

Palmer, Parker J. *A Hidden Wholeness: The Journey Toward an Undivided Life.* San Francisco: Jossey-Bass, 2002.

Weiss, Andrew. *Beginning Mindfulness: Learning the Way of Awareness.* Novato, CA: New World Library, 2004.